RESTARTING
STUDENT WORKBOOK

FOR USE WITH THE RESTARTING DVD SERIES
TWELVE WEEKS COURSE WORKBOOK
Ed Khouri

PART OF
THRIVING: *RECOVER YOUR LIFE*

D1411378

Shepherd's House Inc.
P.O. Box 40096
Pasadena, CA 91114

www.lifemodel.org
www.thrivingrecovery.org

Published by Shepherd's House Inc.
P.O. Box 40096
Pasadena, CA 91114
www.lifemodel.org

ISBN number 978-0-9674357-2-5

KJV Scripture quotations are from: The Holy Bible: King James Version. 1995. Logos Research Systems, Inc.: Oak Harbor, WA.

NKJV Scripture quotations are from: The New King James Version. 1996, 1982, Thomas Nelson: Nashville.

NIV Scripture quotations are from: The Holy Bible, NEW INTERNATIONAL VERSION®. Copyright 1973, 1978, 1984 International Bible Society. All rights reserved throughout the world. Used by permission of International Bible Society.

RSV Scripture quotations are from: The Revised Standard Version. 1971, Logos Research Systems, Inc.: Oak Harbor, WA.

Good News Bible Scripture quotations are from: *The Good News Bible*. 1966, 1971, 1976, American Bible Society: New York, NY.

The Message Scripture quotations are taken from: *The Message*. Copyright 1993, 1994, 1995, 1996, 2000, 2001, 2002. Used by permission of NavPress Publishing Group.

The Twelve Steps are quoted from: *The Anonymous Press Mini-Edition* of Alcoholics Anonymous. The Anonymous Press, 1992, 2005. The inclusion of the Twelve Steps does not mean that A.A. has reviewed or approved the contents of this publication, nor that A.A. agrees with the views expressed in the Restarting video. A.A. is a program of recovery from alcoholism only. Use of the Twelve Steps in contents and discussions which address other matters does not imply otherwise.

Dr. Daniel Amen:
Change Your Brain, Change Your Life, New York, NY: Random House, 1998.
Healing The Hardware Of The Soul, New York, NY: Simon & Schuster, Inc., 2002.

Dr. Allan Schore:
Affect Regulation and the Origin of the Self, Hillsdale, NJ: Erlbaum, 1994.
Affect Regulation And The Repair Of The Self, New York, NY: W. W. Norton & Company, 2003.
Dysregulation And Disorders Of The Self, New York, NY: W. W. Norton & Company, 2003.

TABLE OF CONTENTS

FOREWORD

I am a person in recovery from the pain of trauma and addictions. I know from personal experience what it feels like to be stuck in the pain and shame of life-controlling problems – and not be able to break free. I think this paraphrase from the book of Lamentations describes it best:

How deserted I feel.
I once had friends and people around me, but now I am alone.
My life once mattered to me and to others – my dreams were important,
But now I have become a slave.

I cry – and can't stop feeling empty
Tears run down my cheeks – everyone knows I'm hurting.
The things I found to relieve my pain became my greatest loves,
And now there is no one to comfort me.
My great loves have betrayed me,
My addictions have become my enemy.

My pain and addictions have enslaved me – and rule over me.
I am exhausted.
I have no place to go – nowhere to turn.
The people that once were important to me are gone.
I have no place to rest.
My pain and addictions pursued me, and have overtaken me,
In the midst of the worst moments of my life.

Nothing I do connects me to joy and life.
No one comes when I call for help – or even knows how to help me.
I've done everything I know how to do – and I still am empty, desolate and alone.
The people I thought were my friends hurt just as badly as I do.
There is no one I know who can help me.
Every good thing in me feels dead.

My addictions have become my master.
(Lamentations 1: 1-5, Author's Paraphrase).

I am happy to report that I have been in recovery from trauma and addictions for almost three decades. God has graciously helped me walk into the gift of recovery. I have found freedom from pain and addictions that I never dreamed possible. My heart and dreams are becoming ever more fully alive as I grow and mature in my relationship with Jesus – and with others who are empowered by joy.

One of the dreams that God has placed in my heart is for you.

My dream for you is that you would be able to walk fully into the freedom of recovery – and be empowered by joy to live from the heart and dreams that Jesus has placed within you. You and I have a destiny that is far beyond sobriety and freedom from pain. Our destiny is to become fully alive, connected in joy to God and others in relationships that are life giving. My dream for you is so big, that I believe you will discover the dreams that God has for you – and for others. You can become a source of help, healing and empowering joy for others like us who struggle.

This Restarting workbook is a part of my dream, and it is written for you.

Ed Khouri

ACKNOWLEDGEMENTS

This workbook – and the Restarting project – would not be possible without the help, encouragement and joyful support from many people.

Maritza, you are my joy, love and partner in life. Aside from the fact that you have the most beautiful curly hair and smile of anyone I know, you gave up time with me, and sacrificed what you wanted so that this workbook could be complete. Your input, advice, ideas, creativity and expertise are woven throughout this workbook in patterns that most people will never know. We share the hope that many will be able to walk fully into the joy, life and recovery that we experience together. Your support, care and understanding are what made it possible for me to finish. Thank you, Bellisima!

Jim, you are a blessing. This workbook and project could have never happened without you. The Life Model has changed how I view life and recovery, and it has enriched the relationship that Maritza and I share. Your wisdom, discernment, editing, patience, kindness and boundless joy have fueled this project. When we started out, I never dreamed what Thriving and Restarting could become. It is fun to dream with you!

Jake and Jordan, thanks for giving me the time to write. You are joys to me, and it is my hope that you will walk fully into the destiny that God has placed within your heart.

Deni, you have helped me mature and grow in ways I never knew possible. You are such a delight! You make me proud to be your dad every day.

Christian, you bring me hope for the next generation of recovery leaders.

Tucker, you are truly the Thriving Dog!

Thanks to the Equipping Hearts Board and Vision Team for your support, encouragement and practical advice.

Karl and Charlotte, thank you so much for your gentleness, compassion, faithfulness and perseverance. You never gave up - and never stopped seeking the presence of Jesus. He has given you something extraordinary to share with the world, and thanks to your hard work, the lives of many hurting people are going to be transformed forever through Immanuel Process moments.

Mom and Dad, thanks for loving me enough to teach me to do my best – and to do hard things. You taught me a standard of excellence that has remained with me throughout my life.

I have been blessed with the friendship of many who have taught and mentored me over the years, and to you I am deeply grateful. Thanks to Brian McLaren, Don and Patty Isaac, Jim Isom, Dee Bissel, Mickey Evans and the folks at Dunklin Memorial Camp, Dave Erickson, Ron Ross, Charles and Jean LaCour, David Partington, Alan Smith, Steve Watson, Chris and Jen Coursey, and Bob Jones. There is a part of you all in this project.

RESTARTING
My First 90 Days

WELCOME TO RESTARTING!
A REVOLUTION OF HOPE

Your First 90 Days In Recovery

In the first few days, weeks and months of recovery, our body, brain and emotions are extremely raw. The only things that seem consistent are confusion, and a growing awareness that we are in more pain than we imagined. If you can imagine being knocked unconscious and then tied to the back of a stagecoach – only to wake up as you are being dragged through a cactus patch by a team of 6 galloping horses – then you may be able to understand a little bit of what it is like for those of us suffering from addictions, trauma and abuse to enter recovery. The difference is the length of time our addictions and abuse have plowed through the cactus with us in tow!

All of us wonder how our lives became such a painful mess. Addicted, traumatized and abused were not the kind of plans we dreamed as children. We are usually horrified that we even have to confront or admit these issues. Until our pain got bad enough, we tried to deny the reality of our problem and pain in the hopes that we would be able to ignore or cover up – and just get on with our lives.

What if you could begin to build a new life that is empowered by joy – and not fear, anxiety, addiction, trauma or abuse? What if you could learn new relationship skills that will help you – and those around you thrive? Suppose you could learn practical skills that will help train your brain for sobriety and health as part of a recovery community that is intentional about learning to grow together in joy? You could begin a healing relationship with God that will grow to help you resolve the pain of your addictions, trauma and abuse. You begin the first 90 days of your recovery in the Restarting program!

Restarting will help you "jump-start" your recovery by helping you learn simple exercises that will train your brain for your new life. In each Restarting session, about 2/3 of our time is spent learning exercises that can help change your life! Only about 1/3 is spent on teaching. As you practice each weekly Restarting exercise in group and on your own, you will discover that your brain is beginning to heal from addictions and the devastating effects of trauma and abuse. You will begin to feel the first glimmers of hope as you start to experience the new warmth and sensations of joy – and lay an entirely new foundation for your life. Instead of ongoing pain, dread and dissatisfaction, you will find that your relationships with God and others are becoming a source of joy, hope and healing. And, since Restarting contains a solution-centered approach to recovery combined with teaching that is based on current new research about recovery and the brain, you will also find many of the answers to your questions about addiction, trauma and abuse – and how they have affected your life.

MY FIRST 90 DAYS
RESTARTING

Restarting from substance addictions or a life-crisis. As soon as your head begins to clear and your body starts to feel better, you are ready to start. The distress and disruption from early-stage withdrawal, intoxication or intense emotional crisis are simply too great to allow normal brain functioning. As a result, it is a good idea to wait a few days until the acute stages of intoxication, withdrawal or major life crisis have passed until beginning to brain train in Restarting. Learning new joy, relationship, healing and recovery skills means that you need to attend Restarting with a brain that can be trained!

If you are in the early stages of withdrawal or crisis, you are welcome to participate in a crisis group until you are ready for brain training. Not every Thriving Recovery Your Life program will have a crisis unit if the program is still young. The crisis unit is designed to help you stabilize, so that you will be able to begin building joy, relationship and new healing skills as soon as possible!

If you arrive at a Restarting class under the influence of alcohol or other drugs your Restarting Facilitator may ask you to do one of two things: First, if a Thriving Crisis Unit is available, you may be asked to join that group for the day. Second, if you are highly intoxicated, or if no Crisis Unit is available, you will be asked to return home – and come back to group next week ready to train!

What is different about Restarting, and what can I expect to learn in my first 90 days of recovery?

Restarting is designed to help keep you safe. Restarting gives you the opportunity to start rebuilding your life in a community that is very intentional about building joy – and protecting you as you begin your journey. You will practice all of your Restarting exercises in groups of 3-5 people, so that you will not have to build intense one-on-one relationships with people that you don't know. We'll also spend a lot of time helping you discover exactly what healthy relationships look like – and help teach you the skills you need to transform your relationships. You are encouraged to bring a support person with you to Restarting if you have one.

Your trauma memories are private. In Restarting, you don't have to worry about, "What will everyone think about me if I share this?" because you will never be asked to share your deepest wounds, hurt and pain with others. You are not required or even encouraged to disclose your trauma experiences in a Restarting group. You will watch Immanuel healing moments on the video but these are to show you how deep healing for loss (attachment pain) is achieved. You will not be expected to expose your pain or trauma in groups. Instead, we focus on learning and applying solutions to our problems so that we can all grow and mature together.

Restarting is solution-centered. Our primary focus in Restarting is on helping you learn the skills that you need to change your life – and not on discussing and describing the pain that has damaged our life. In Restarting, you will find that approximately 2/3 of each session is centered on helping you learn and practice new recovery skills. These skills train your brain for recovery in a way that discussion of problems can never accomplish. In Restarting, you will discover that we want to grow bonds with you that are built on joyful relationships and solutions – and not centered in our pain and problems.

You will learn how to live a life of joy…and not pain. One of the most devastating effects of addiction, trauma, abuse and painful relationships is that these damage our ability to feel a reasonable amount of pleasure in life. We end up spending most of our time trying to manage, avoid or medicate our pain – and that is a lot of work! In Restarting, you will discover how to train your brain – for a life that is fueled by joy. You are designed to live in joy, and you will discover that the greatest source of joy can be healthy relationships with God and with others. From your first day in Restarting, you will have plenty of opportunities to learn and practice exercises that help you build joy in these relationships.

You will learn how to rest when you are upset. When we have experienced pain in addiction, trauma or abuse, it is probable that we lack the ability to rest – and quiet our mental, emotional, physical and spiritual distress. A brain that does not know how to rest can become very agitated and toxic, and is easily triggered into relapse and other unhealthy behaviors that hurt us and others. In Restarting, you will learn simple skills like breathing and body relaxation that help you calm down. And, as you learn to connect with God, when you are upset, you will find a source of peace that will help you rest.

Avoid relapse by learning to handle intense positive and negative emotions. Almost half of all relapse from substance abuse is caused by positive or negative emotions that are simply too intense and too overwhelming. Because our brain isn't trained to reconnect with others in joy when we are upset, relapse, and a whole variety of frustrating behaviors are the inevitable result. In Restarting, you will learn what your brain needs when you are upset so that you can learn to live – and stay connected to joy.

Learn what healthy relationships look like. Because Restarting exercises focus a lot on building joy in healthy relationships, you will spend weeks discovering the differences between healthy attachments with God and others – and those that cause pain. You will also begin to practice exercises that can help transform your relationships, and learn to stop self-defeating patterns of relationships fueled by attachment pain.

MY FIRST 90 DAYS
RESTARTING

Learn skills to help you recognize and recover from trauma and abuse. Restarting is different, because we are intentional about healing from the devastation of trauma and abuse. Living with the consequences of trauma and abuse make life very painful – and research indicates that trauma is a major factor in the development of addictions. When we live in ongoing pain because of the effects of different types of trauma and abuse, we tend to medicate our pain somehow. In Restarting, you will learn to build the joyful capacity you need to begin to address issues of trauma. You will also begin learning the Immanuel Process, which helps you connect with God in a way that will help you talk with Him about the painful areas of life so that He can bring healing to you.

Find answers to your questions about addiction and co-dependency. Understanding how we become trapped in self-destructive relationships and addictions is an important aspect of Restarting. You will discover the keys you need to break these destructive cycles, and start training your brain for secure, joy-filled relationships that make life feel worth living!

Grow your maturity – and find a blueprint for life. The last 2 sessions of Restarting will help you learn the relationship between maturity – and recovery. You will explore stages of personal maturity, and find out how growing maturity can help prevent relapse into harmful cycles of addiction and other behaviors that are driven by trauma and abuse. You'll also discover a roadmap for growing your own maturity.

Avoid other addictions. In recovery, it is not unusual for people who are driven by pain to switch addictions – or exchange one harmful behavior for another. Because Restarting emphasizes brain training that teaches new recovery skills and helps your brain receive what it really needs, you will be less likely to exchange one pain-driven behavior for another. And, because Restarting helps you begin to address and heal from the trauma and abuse that drive many addictive behaviors – your brain is less likely to find new addictions to medicate pain.

Restarting is training. Everyone struggling to recover from trauma or addictions is missing some basic relational brain skills. Training means teaching your brain and body to do things they don't know how to do and improving how well you do the things you know already. Training can be a little stretch outside your comfort zone. Our brains tend to view new things as not that important and sometimes make us nervous thinking about new things we don't understand very well. How much your brain will actually change during Thriving Recovery Your Life will depend on how much you can practice new skills that do not feel that important to you at first. The skills you will learn here are not too difficult but you will need to practice them many times. Each repetition gives you more skill.

Your second 90 days

When you have completed Restarting in your first 90 days, you are ready for the next module in the Thriving: Recover Your Life Program, which is called Belonging. In Belonging, you will be able to spend 3 months continuing to build joy and growing in recovery and relationship skills. Belonging is training for your brain's control system. You will learn:

- How can I create a place for others to belong in joy around me…and develop life-giving relationships?

- How do I experience appreciation and self-quieting.

- What keeps me alone – and keeps me from creating a place for others to belong with me?

- How can I keep the relational part of my brain working so that I am able to actually connect with God and others.

- How can I practically restore my relational circuits if they are not working well?

- Why do people like – or hate – me, and what can I do about it?

- How do I recognize and deal with the pain that makes me relapse into addictive or abuse driven behaviors…before I relapse?

- What are the skills I need to make my cravings stop in their tracks?

- How can I see my life and others like God does?

- What do I do when I feel overwhelmed by others so that I calm down quickly?

- How can I learn to respond well to others…and not overwhelm or ignore them?

MY FIRST 90 DAYS
RESTARTING

What comes next?

Your third 90 days you will be spend in the Healing module. You need time to learn to heal. This training helps you experience the presence of God in a way that helps you heal from the devastating effects of addictions, trauma, neglect and abuse. In Healing, you will work in small groups to continue to learn and practice the Immanuel Process. You will discover:

- How can I connect with God to talk with Him about my pain?

- How can unhappy memories silently block my awareness of God?

- What steps can I take to resolve these problems?

- Why does God want to connect with me anyway?

- What can I do when I get stuck working through something painful in my life?

- How can I learn to help others begin to talk with God about their pain?

- How can I learn to have a more stable identity, even when things are going wrong?

- How can we as a group all heal, grow and move forward in joy together?

Finishing your first year in recovery – the last 90 days

The Loving module will help you to apply practically all you have learned in the Thriving Program. Your focus is growing relationships with the people in your life that you care about the most. You will work on the skills needed to:

- Build relationships that help my recovery.

- Remove the fear that keeps me from relating to those closest to me.

- Create a place for those I care about to belong with me in joy.

- Know how attachment pain has kept me from relating to those I care about.

- Know what do when relationships don't heal.

- Continue to connect with God to resolve ongoing pain in my relationships.

Wait…there is more!

At the end of your first year in recovery, you will want to share your new life – and joy – with others, and may want to invite others to go through the program with you again. This will help you and the people you love to build joy, relationship and healing skills that you can share together. Stronger joy bonds are an essential part of recovery, and going through the Thriving: Recover Your Life program again with others is a good way to build strong relationships. In your second year you strengthen your skills. Strong skills are important for staying joyful.

After 2 years, you may even discover that you want to help others recover from their pain – and begin to help volunteer for training in a Thriving group. You can share the joy you've found to help others begin their recovery journey!

WELCOME TO RESTARTING!
A REVOLUTION OF HOPE

You And I Are Created For Joy!
Joy-filled attachments to God and to others create joy in us, and help our brains learn to regulate emotion, pain and pleasure effectively. Synchronized relationships actually teach our brains to regulate dopamine (which helps us feel joy) and serotonin (which helps us quiet ourselves). In this way, we can learn to return to joy from negative emotions and develop secure attachments with God and others that are life giving. We feel alive, fulfilled – energized by the power of joy!

The Problem: A Lack Of Joyful Brain Training
Research strongly suggests that when our relationships with God and others are not joyful, the brain lacks the ability to effectively regulate emotions or consistently feel pleasure. We do not learn to live in joy, quiet ourselves when we are upset, or learn to handle negative emotions. We live in painful states that our brains have not learned to regulate internally. This lack of joyful brain training affects life from infancy – throughout adulthood.

Our capacity to connect with others in life giving relationships is one area greatly damaged by our lack of capacity for joy. Without a brain that is trained to attach to others in joy, our attachments with others seem to only perpetuate our pain. Relationships – that are designed by God to be a source of life and joy – become painful and sometimes toxic. This is highly painful and very traumatic – particularly when we didn't have much capacity to regulate negative emotions already. We tend to be locked in unending cycles of pain and broken relationships. Our pain feels unbearable.

Stuck in pain, and without joyful relationships with God and others, our brain lacks the skills and the attachments that are necessary to learn to regulate negative emotions and live in joy. The brain simply is unable to regulate our distress effectively. Lacking the joyful attachments with God and others that could help retrain it, our brain craves other attachments that might help medicate our pain. Addiction is the process by which the brain attaches to Behaviors, Events, Experiences, People and Substances (BEEPS) so that it can regulate emotion, increase pleasure and decrease pain.

Once our brain attaches itself to BEEPS, these attachments literally rewire our brain and alter the way it functions. In essence, BEEPS hijack the emotional control center of the brain responsible for attachment, emotional control and decision-making. When BEEPS are behind the wheel, they drive our lives and relationships to places of even greater pain.

The Search For Help
In desperation, we looked for help. We've tried support groups, counseling or treatment programs. We felt better, because caring people listened to our problems. "Talking things over" seemed to help – at least for a while, and we may have even changed our behaviors for a time. Inside, however, we were often left with a nagging sense that there was more to life than simply "not doing the wrong thing." Our relationships were still difficult, our joy capacity was low, and we struggled with difficult emotions.

Sometimes, we simply exchanged one problem behavior for another, or relapsed back into our addictions. We still needed BEEPS, because our brain was still unable to regulate our emotions, pain and pleasure effectively. We may have simply exchanged primary attachments to overtly destructive BEEPS such as alcohol or other illegal drugs to more hidden BEEPS such as work, perfection or food. We may have changed codependent relationships – but still felt empty, lost and frustrated on the inside. Our behaviors changed, but because

WELCOME TO RESTARTING!
A REVOLUTION OF HOPE

our brain had not learned to regulate emotions, pleasure and pain effectively, it still sought and found external attachments to medicate our distress. Our brain was still not sober.

Some of us turned to God and to the church for help. We longed for a deep sense of connection that could change our level of pain. Some of us were disappointed when the "quick fix" we hoped for did not come. We found that trying to do "the right things" to change, fit in and be accepted did not significantly change the pain and struggles we felt on the inside. Sometimes, we were frustrated because "God's people" did not seem to understand – or want to understand – our problems. When the spiritual or biblical advice they gave us did not bring about the promised "quick fix," some may even have blamed us for the failure and pulled away. We felt worse – not better.

At times, we were able to connect with others in God's family who genuinely cared for us, but simply did not know how to help us. They did not know that we were stuck because our brain had not learned to regulate our emotions effectively – and they did not know how to retrain our brain in joy. They cared – but caring was not enough. In our pain, we cried out, "God, is this the best you can do?" In our distress, we heard no answer – and concluded that God, and His people had no answers for us either. It was just one more experience in a long line of failures and disappointments.

Across The Line Of Despair

We tried secular and spiritual solutions, and still felt empty, frustrated, alone, and ashamed of our struggles and behaviors. In spite of sincere attempts to find help – and the sincere attempts of others to help us – we were unable to find lasting relief for our internal pain. Long-term solutions for our problem behaviors or addictions were beyond our reach. Even God seemed distant and without answers. We had no hope – but plenty of pain, shame and relationships that did not bring us joy. We had crossed the line of despair into hopelessness and rage.

When we cross the line of despair, many of us react differently. Since our brain has not been adequately trained to regulate our internal distress, our behaviors tend to be driven by pain and hopelessness. Some of us lash out at others, and take our frustrations out on the people closest to us. This not only hurts them – it hurts us as well. At times, despair may drive us further into self-destructive attachments with BEEPS. We may plunge back into our original addictions – or find new ones to numb our pain. Sometimes, we simply lapse into apathy and hopeless despair. We haven't been able to find solutions that work – and feel too hopeless to try anymore.

Restarting: A Revolution of Hope

We need a revolution of hope! The word revolution means, "a dramatic change in ideas or practice" (Microsoft Encarta Dictionary). We need a "dramatic change in our ideas and practice" about recovery that can bring us realistic hope of change. This is what Restarting is all about.

Restarting offers a solution-centered approach to recovery and change that is not focused on describing or talking about your problem in new or different ways. Restarting can help you lay a new foundation for change by helping you retrain your brain as you develop relationships with God and with others who are empowered by joy. In Restarting, you will learn simple joy and relationship building skills that help teach your brain to regulate emotions, pleasure and pain more effectively.

Restarting also is an opportunity to revolutionize your experience with God – and receive

WELCOME TO RESTARTING!
A REVOLUTION OF HOPE

healing from deep wounds and trauma from the past. Restarting will teach you simple exercises that help you experience the presence of Jesus in a way that is life giving and healing. Developing a conscious awareness of Jesus' presence keeps us in constant touch with the joy of One who is always glad to be with us.

Restarting also will give you the opportunity to become part of a community that is building joy together. You will find the support, joy and maturity you need to mature in the context of the life-giving relationships that can continue throughout the Thriving: Recover Your Life program. You will find yourself becoming more fully alive than you ever dreamed possible!

We Can Learn Practical Joy-Building, Relationship and Inner Healing Skills
Building joy in the context of secure, healthy relationships with God and others helps change our brain. As we learn to build joy and then experience quiet together with others, we are better able to regulate positive and negative emotions, pleasure and pain. As our capacity for joy grows, we are better able to respond to the stresses of life, without being overwhelmed.

Our increasing capacity for joy also allows us to form attachments and relationships with others that are secure. Our relationships become characterized by joy and mutual satisfaction. We are increasingly able to stay connected with each other when we are upset, and find that, instead of destroying our relationships, these challenges actually strengthen our bond with God and others. Joy is helping us choose attachments that are life-giving.

Our increasing capacity is also allowing us to begin to resolve painful life issues from our past. As we learn to experience the presence of Jesus, we find that He is able to bring hope and healing to the damaged and wounded areas of our hearts. He changes and heals us – from the inside out.

We Can Be Free From Attachments to BEEPS
As joy builds and our attachments and bonds with God and others become healthy, we find that unhealthy attachments to BEEPS become increasingly less important. Because our brain is being re-trained to regulate pain, pleasure and emotions in the context of joyful relationships with others, our brain is learning to handle our internal distress more effectively. It no longer needs BEEPS to medicate our pain. We find that we are increasingly able to live in the power of joy that gives us strength, transforms our lives, and helps us to grow into all that Jesus has created us to be.

Welcome to the Restarting Revolution
As you read this workbook, you will find that it is written for you. By reading through each chapter, you will find out more about how your Restarting workbook is organized – and how your life can be transformed by the power of joy. Welcome to the revolution!

WELCOME TO RESTARTING!
HOW CAN I USE MY WORKBOOK?

You will need your workbook for every session of Restarting, so be sure to bring it with you to group. You will also need a pen or pencil to take notes or complete worksheets.

You will cover one chapter in your workbook each week. Each Restarting session includes a Restarting video as well as the exercises and material located in your workbook. Each chapter of your workbook contains:

- A complete list of everything that will be covered in your weekly Restarting group session.
- Instructions for each weekly exercise.
- Teaching notes from your weekly Restarting video.
- Questions for further study.
- 12 Step questions for further study.
- Worksheets to help you complete Restarting group exercises.

During your Restarting group, you will have the opportunity to participate in many group exercises. Detailed instructions for each exercise are listed in each chapter, and your facilitator will go over these instructions with you. You are welcome to ask questions about anything that is unclear or that you do not understand. For some exercises, you will need worksheets that you will find in each chapter in which they are required.

Your workbook also contains teaching notes that accompany the video. Those of you who like to take notes will be relieved to find that every bit of text seen on the DVD is printed in outline form in your workbook. Each page of your workbook contains space for you to take notes.

You will also find it helpful to answer the questions at the end of each chapter. These questions are designed to function as study guides, and help you better understand and apply the most important concepts from each chapter and video. Because the questions are based on the weekly videos and group exercises, you will have to attend your Restarting group to best answer the questions. The teaching notes in your workbook will help you.

You do not have to complete the answers to these questions – they are for your growth and study only, and your regular weekly Restarting group will not discuss the questions. In some cases, your facilitator may offer Restarting study groups that will meet on other nights of the week to discuss the questions.

WELCOME TO RESTARTING!
GOD AND RESTARTING

From all credible reports, God is alive – and thriving! Because He has created us in His image, we have the same possibility: becoming fully alive in Him. This is the goal of Restarting - to be made fully alive in Him, flowing in the easy rhythm of the Spirit, and empowered to fulfill the unique purposes for which God has created us. Restarting, and the entire Thriving: Recover Your Life training flow begins and ends with this purpose.

Restarting teaches us that we are created in the image and likeness of God – and that means that we are created for joyful loving relationships with Him and others. In the context of joyful and loving relationships, our brains are trained according to their original design. By experiencing these joyful, synchronized relationships in the first two years of life, we are empowered to develop relationships with God and others that are secure and life giving. We are free to begin to discover our unique gifts and talents. The unique facets of our individual design, gifts and heart will be revealed when we connect in joyful relationships with God and others.

We develop an identity that is strong and healthy. We become rooted and grounded in love. The bonds we form with others – and with God – are joyful and life giving. Our group identity is strong and honoring to God. We are free to mature and grow according to the full capacity of our individual design. Our relationships with others are marked by healthy interdependence as together we are able to fulfill the purpose for which God's family is created.

We bring life wherever we go, and take the joy of secure attachments to places they've never been. We serve others and steward the life, resources and gifts we've been given. We can enjoy pleasure as God intended. We become family to those who are alone and care for their needs as the family of God. This is the vision of healthy relationships that Restarting is designed to help fulfill.

This is a work that begins and ends in the hope that is in Jesus.

Why are so many of us stuck in the pain of trauma and addiction? We want to be free – but we can't seem to make it past our past! To those of us who yearn for hope, Restarting offers you a revolutionary idea: You can be free!

What keeps us from flowing easily in joyful and quieting rhythms of grace? God has designed our brains so that they can be transformed – trained for joy, relationship and life until the day we die. We are never too old for relationships with Him and others that heal. Restarting offers participants an opportunity to encounter and experience the joyful and life giving relationships with God and others that can call our hearts back to life. In the context of a joyful, healing community, we can learn new skills that build our capacity for joy, learn to quiet ourselves and return to joy from negative emotions, and develop relationships with others that help us to heal. This is what God has known all along, we need to be connected with Him and with His family to thrive.

In addition, Restarting teaches us to perceive, experience and learn to live in the moment by moment awareness of the presence of Jesus. The Bible calls this "living by the Spirit." His life and presence bring fullness of joy, hope and healing. In Restarting, you will have the opportunity to learn simple prayer exercises that help you learn to experience the presence of Jesus. Because Jesus is Lord of All – past, present and future – He can heal our painful wounds from the past.

Restarting is about beginning a new life in recovery that is full of hope and freedom. If you are suffering from the painful experience of trauma, or unhealthy attachments to Behaviors, Events, Experiences, People or Substances – Restarting offers you a new opportunity to walk more fully into your destiny. As your heart is healing, you will find that you are becoming more fully alive. You are awakening to the possibilities of the dreams that God has dreamed for you.

RESTARTING GROUP
GROUND RULES

Wise Thoughts About Group Rules

1. You can help build joy and a recovery community for you and others. Your community thrives when you keep the personal information Restarting members share in your group confidential. Do not share it with others. Your facilitator will help you and others stay safe by reporting child or elder abuse – and any imminent danger to you or to the person or property of others.

2. Take every opportunity to build joy – and practice your joy-building skills in Restarting.

3. Express appreciation to each other frequently.

4. When you are glad to be with others, it helps them feel like they belong – and helps build a Restarting community that is joyful.

5. Supportive listening helps others share, heal and feel comfortable. It's a lot harder for others to build joy with you when you are offering criticism or advice. The directions that accompany each exercise will help you learn to offer constructive and helpful feedback that builds joy.

6. Sharing is strongly encouraged, but not required.

7. By following your facilitator's instructions and the directions in your workbook, you will help keep your group on track, learn new Restarting skills, and help provide enough time for everyone to share.

8. Encourage others to return to Restarting.

9. Following your facilitator's directions to complete all Restarting exercises in groups of 3-5 people will help you build the kind of joy that is powerful – and safe – for you and everyone else.

10. It is very difficult for you and for others to create belonging if you arrive for group intoxicated, so if you come to group "under the influence", you won't be able to participate in Restarting that evening.

11. Threats, violence and intimidation are a sign that you are overwhelmed – and are actively and intensely overwhelming others. Because these behaviors make Restarting unsafe for others, you will be unable to return to Restarting if you do them.

RESTARTING
WORKBOOK

FOR USE WITH THE RESTARTING DVD SERIES
TWELVE WEEKS COURSE WORKBOOK

1 TRAIN YOUR BRAIN FOR A CHANGE
HOW IS THE BRAIN ORGANIZED? WHAT DOES IT NEED?

OPEN THE GROUP WITH PRAYER

APPRECIATION EXERCISE: *10-15 Minutes*

1. Break into small groups of 3-5 people.

2. Your facilitator will explain that this exercise has several purposes:
   a. This exercise helps build joy and relationship skills.
   b. This exercise helps activate the right orbital prefrontal cortex of your brain. Activation of this area of the brain is essential for learning.

3. Your facilitator will ask you to think about a person that you appreciate and a time you felt especially grateful to be with that person.

4. Your facilitator will share with you about his or her special person for one minute.

As your facilitator shares, he/she will:
   a. Maintain eye contact while sharing.
   b. Identify the person he/she appreciates, and describe a moment when he/she was especially grateful to be with them.
   c. Describe the emotions he/she felt while he/she was with them.
   d. Describe what his/her body felt like when he/she was with them.

5. Your facilitator will remind you of a few guidelines for this exercise:
   a. All Restarting exercises are done in groups of 3-5 people.
   b. Sharing in small group is strongly encouraged, but is not required.
   c. Support each other through active listening and appropriate eye contact.
   d. Please do not offer comments, criticism or advice in response to what others have shared.

6. Your facilitator will ask volunteers to each share for one minute about the person they appreciate. As you share, be sure to:
   a. Maintain appropriate eye contact while sharing. Remember, this exercise is joy-building – not a staring contest!
   b. Identify the person you appreciate, and describe a moment when you were especially grateful to be with them.
   c. Describe what emotions you felt while you were with them.
   d. Describe what your body felt like when you were with them.

7. When each group is finished, your facilitator may ask volunteers to share with the entire group how they felt before and after the exercise. Use one or two words to describe your feelings.

TRAIN YOUR BRAIN FOR A CHANGE
HOW IS THE BRAIN ORGANIZED? WHAT DOES IT NEED?

TODAY´S LESSON: How is the Brain Organized? What Does It Need?

CLASS NOTES: How is the Brain Organized? What Does it Need?

How are we created?
- Then God said, "Let Us make man in Our image, according to Our likeness... Then God saw everything that He had made, and indeed it was very good.

  Genesis 1:26, 31. NKJV.

  Let us: God is relational!
  Make man in our image: created by God in his image and his likeness - relational.
  It was very good: God was really happy with the way we turned out.
- We function according to our original design – like God when we are in relationship with Him and with each other.

We are designed so that our brain functions best in secure relationships!
- I will praise You, for I am fearfully and wonderfully made; Marvelous are your works, and that my soul knows very well. Psalm 139:14, NKJV.

The brain is created with 2 hemispheres
- The 2 hemispheres are different.
- They are designed to work together.
- The brain works best when each side is healthy and they are synchronized together.

Left and right
- Left side: naming and explaining
- Right side: knowing and experiencing

The left hemisphere
- A place of words and language
- A place of stories
- A place of descriptions
- A place of explanations, logic and reasoning
- Very resistant to change
- Persists in the face of contrary evidence
- Open to change only when the right hemisphere is "upset"

The right hemisphere
- Non-verbal
- Imagistic
- Prosodic (voice tone)
- Executive control system of the brain
- Contains a four-level emotional brain structure
- Dominant for emotions and body
- Synchronizes and notices "everything"
- Decides when the left hemisphere can change beliefs

TRAIN YOUR BRAIN FOR A CHANGE
HOW IS THE BRAIN ORGANIZED? WHAT DOES IT NEED?

In the right brain: a four level control center
- *Level One:*
  - Attachment
  - Thalamus and basal ganglia, help regulate dopamine
- *Level Two:*
  - The guardshack: life is good, bad or scary
  - The amygdala: helps regulate adrenaline
- *Level Three:*
  - Synchronization
  - The cingulate cortex: helps regulate serotonin
  - Helps resolve negative emotions
- *Level Four:*
  - Identity
  - The right orbital prefrontal cortex
  - Helps me focus my attention, and answer the question "Who am I?"

Relationships are the building blocks for healthy brains
- The right brain's emotional control center develops from birth.
- Level 1 attachment is the foundation for this growth.
- A healthy control center allows the right brain and the later developing left brain to be synchronized and have healthy connections.
- Relationships are the foundation for the development and integration of the entire brain!

Dr. Allan Schore
- Affect Regulation and Origin of the Self
- Affect Regulation and the Repair of the Self
- Affect Dysregulation and Disorders of the Self

For healthy development, the brain needs joyful relationships.

Joy means relationships!

Joy means: we are glad to be together. Someone is glad to be with me!

Right-hemisphere to right-hemisphere communication
- Right brain > left face > left side of retinas > right brain
- Six complete cycles of communication every second
- Synchronized brain chemistry
- Matched brain structure growth
- Authentic, truthful, rapid communication
- Emotions are AMPLIFIED each cycle
- Subjectively experienced as produced by the "other"

Climbing Joy Mountain: capacity

When our joy capacity is low, life is painful.
- The deepest level of pain is attachment pain at level 1 of the control center.

TRAIN YOUR BRAIN FOR A CHANGE
HOW IS THE BRAIN ORGANIZED? WHAT DOES IT NEED?

Medicate to regulate

BEEPS
- BEEPS are attachments to Behaviors, Events, Experiences, People or Substances that are used to regulate emotions, increase pleasure or decrease pain.

BEEPS
- Attachments to BEEPS help us medicate – to artificially regulate – positive and negative emotions as well as pain.

BEEPS
- Attachments to BEEPS take the place of secure attachments to God and significant others.

BEEPS
- There are many different types of BEEPS.
- Behaviors: Work
- Events: Thrill Seeking
- Experiences: Sex
- People: Relationships
- Substances: Alcohol

Thriving and the Twelve Steps
- Since the 1930's Twelve Step and self-help groups have helped millions of men and women around the world find hope and sobriety.
- Thriving, through the advances in research made in "The Decade of the Brain," is a program designed to help participants become healthy, whole, sober and mature.
- Thriving teaches participants the joy and relationship building skills that the brain needs to heal – and remain sober – through the development of secure, healthy attachments with God and others in a mature, life-giving community.

BEEPS promise relief but make life unmanageable
- Step 1: We admitted we were powerless over BEEPS – that our lives had become unmanageable.

BEEPS attachments are sub-cortical
- BEEPS affect the attachment center of the brain.
- The brain is designed so that dopamine and endogenous opiates are released when people are "glad to be with us."
- This is the neurochemistry of joy!

BEEPS fool the attachment center
- BEEPS also trigger the release of dopamine and stimulate the pleasure center of the brain.
- BEEPS mimic genuine joyful relationships.
- In this way, the attachment center is fooled into attaching to BEEPS to regulate every single emotion, pleasure and pain.

TRAIN YOUR BRAIN FOR A CHANGE
HOW IS THE BRAIN ORGANIZED? WHAT DOES IT NEED?

BEEPS hijack the attachment center
- The attachment center learns to rely on BEEPS – and not relationships with God and others that produce joy.
- In this way, BEEPS hijack the attachment center.
- When BEEPS take over, life becomes unmanageable – we end up in places we never wanted to go.

Recovering our life means becoming connected in joyful relationships with God and with other people.

And that is why we need joy & relationships!

EXERCISE: The Father Wound Video Discussion: *20-25 Minutes*
After watching Rocky in the "Father Wound Video"

1. Break into groups of 3-5 people.

2. Volunteers may share answers to the following questions about the video:
   a. What was your impression of how different Rocky looked during the session and then at follow-up?
   b. What was the difference in Rocky's life after the session with Dr. Lehman?
   c. How did you feel when you watched Rocky's video?
   d. In the video, Rocky experienced Jesus being "glad to be with him" at a very painful moment of his life. Why was this important for Rocky?
   e. What happened to Rocky's attachment to food?
   f. Do you think this healing process can be important for our own recovery from trauma and attachments to BEEPS?

3. Your facilitator will remind you to:
   a. Stay relational by making appropriate eye contact as you share.
   b. Support each other by actively listening as others share.
   c. Please do not give advice or offer criticism or corrective comments about what others have shared.

4. Your facilitator will help you by keeping track of time.

5. Following the small group sharing, your facilitator may ask volunteers to share their insights and responses with the entire group. (Approximately 10 minutes.)

CLOSE THE GROUP WITH PRAYER

THRIVING RECOVER YOUR LIFE
HOW DO THE FIVE THRIVING MODULES WORK TOGETHER?

MODULES

Restarting

Restarting is the entry module for the *Thriving: Recover Your Life* program. Over a 12 week period, in Restarting groups you learn how you are created for joy. You learn how to recognize where your brain lacks joy and how to connect with others in order to retrain your brain FOR JOY! Restarting groups combine joy building exercises, DVD teachings from Ed Khouri and this workbook full of notes, follow up questions and 12 Step applications for training. Each class is one third teaching and two thirds exercises! Restarting is all about retraining the brain, not just understanding why we are the way we are!

Forming

Thriving is for the whole church. Forming is an entrance to the Thriving: Recover your life program for people who want to grow their spiritual maturity by engaging at deeper levels with God. This 12 week module is all about forming your relationship with Jesus! In Forming, you will learn more about hearing God and finding your true identity in Christ. You will begin to see yourself through the eyes of heaven and recognize grace as an active force for change.

Belonging

Your second 90 days take you through the Belonging module. You will work in small groups to restore your ability to create a joyful place for others to belong with you. Belonging jump-starts your process of learning the 19 skills that build healthy relationships and strong emotional resilience. In Belonging you learn to recognize when your relational circuits are off and get them running again. Creating belonging means learning not to overwhelm others, recognizing the effects of attachment pain and learning a surprising way to control your cravings.

Healing

Healing is the module where you can discover how to experience Jesus in the painful places of life. Jesus is the healer, and by the time participants get to this module, they have built up enough joy capacity to let Jesus do His work! We work on inner healing in the safety of groups of 3 to 5 and begin each exercise with God in a joyful situation! In Healing, we will learn to distinguish God's voice from our own. This module will utilize the Immanuel Process developed in connection with Dr. Karl Lehman.

Loving

Loving is the last module in Thriving: Recover Your Life. In this module you will take what you have learned in all the previous modules and apply it to your own relationships. You will take the joy and healing that you have been developing back to the relationships that God has placed in your life. You will practice receiving and giving good things to the people you live with and love - or wish you could.

TRAIN YOUR BRAIN FOR A CHANGE
HOW IS THE BRAIN ORGANIZED? WHAT DOES IT NEED?

QUESTIONS FOR FURTHER DISCUSSION OR FOLLOW-UP

1. How did God create our brains, and why do we need relationships?

2. What are the dominant functions of the *left hemisphere* of the brain?

3. What are the dominant functions of the *right hemisphere* of the brain?

4. Where is the *four level control center* located, and why is it important?

5. What does the brain need for healthy development?

6. What is joy?

7. Why is it important to build increasing joy capacity?

8. What happens when our joy capacity is low?

9. What are BEEPS, and why are they important?

10. Did you recognize attachments to BEEPS in your own life?

11. Did you recognize attachments to BEEPS in the lives of important people in your life, such as family members and friends?

12. How do BEEPS hijack the attachment center of my brain, and why do BEEPS make my life unmanageable?

13. What do I need to recover my life?

TRAIN YOUR BRAIN FOR A CHANGE
HOW IS THE BRAIN ORGANIZED? WHAT DOES IT NEED?

OPTIONAL 12 STEP QUESTIONS

1. What was the first BEEPS you ever used?

2. What other BEEPS have you used?

3. What are your BEEPS attachments now?

4. What happened the first time you used BEEPS? What did you feel like before and after?

5. What happened the last time you used BEEPS?

6. How have your attachments to BEEPS caused you problems in relationships?
   Have you ever damaged or lost a relationship through your attachments to BEEPS?
   Think about relationships with your parents, brothers & sisters, spouse, children, family and close friends.

7. Have your attachments with BEEPS ever caused you problems with work?
   Have you ever lost a job or gotten in trouble for use of BEEPS at work?
   Think about issues like being late for work or missing work because of BEEPS use. Have you ever used BEEPS on the job – or at lunch?

8. Have your attachments to BEEPS ever gotten you in legal trouble?

9. How have attachments to BEEPS impacted your physical health?

10. Have you lost things you valued as a result of your attachments to BEEPS? Think about things like: relationships, jobs, health, houses, cars, values, dignity and respect.

11. How have your attachments to BEEPS affected the way you feel about yourself? How do you feel when you think about how BEEPS have affected your life and relationships?

12. On a scale of 1 (lowest) – 10 (highest), describe how painful BEEPS attachments have been in your life.

13. Have you ever tried to give up an attachment to BEEPS? What happened?

14. Do you think that BEEPS have hijacked part of your life?

15. What do the words powerless and unmanageability mean to you?

2 THE 2 SKILLS YOUR BRAIN CAN'T LIVE WITHOUT
THE RHYTHMS OF JOY AND QUIET

OPEN THE GROUP WITH PRAYER

YOUR NOTES

APPRECIATION EXERCISE: *5 Minutes*

1. Break into small groups of 3-5 people.

2. Your facilitator will explain that this exercise has several purposes.
   a. This exercise helps build joy and relationship skills.
   b. This exercise helps activate the right orbital prefrontal cortex of your brain. Activation of this area of the brain is essential for learning.

3. Your facilitator will ask you to think about an experience in the past week in which you felt appreciation for someone or something.

4. Your facilitator will take one minute to share his/her appreciation moment with you. He/she will:
   a. Maintain eye contact while sharing.
   b. Describe the appreciation experience, person or moment.
   c. Describe what emotions they felt during that experience.
   d. Describe what their body felt like during that experience.

5. Your facilitator will remind you of a few simple guidelines for this exercise:
   a. Sharing in a small group is strongly encouraged, but is not required.
   b. Support each other through active listening and appropriate eye contact.
   c. Please do not offer comments, criticism or advice in response to what others have shared.

6. Your facilitator will ask volunteers to each share for one minute about the person or moment that they appreciate. As you share, remember to:
   a. Maintain appropriate eye contact while sharing. Remember, this is a joy building exercise – not a staring contest!
   b. Describe the person or experience you appreciate.
   c. Describe what emotions you felt during that experience.
   d. Describe what your body felt like during that experience.

7. When each group is finished, your facilitator may ask volunteers to share with the entire group how they felt before and after the exercise. Volunteers should use one or two words to describe their feelings.

THE 2 SKILLS YOUR BRAIN CAN´T LIVE WITHOUT
THE RHYTHMS OF JOY AND QUIET

YOUR NOTES

EXERCISE: LEARN TO RELAX AND BREATHE DEEPLY *10 Minutes.*

1. Before beginning this exercise, your facilitator will advise you that:

   a. If you are concerned about your physical ability to do this exercise, or if you have any spine, bone or muscle injury, weakness or problem, please consult with your doctor before attempting this exercise.

   b. The breathing portions of this exercise may be done while seated, and can be practiced without the muscle relaxation segments of this exercise.

2. Please follow your facilitator's instructions as you do this exercise.

3. Stand up, and make sure that you have 3-4 feet of clear space around you.

4. Imagine that you are a marionette – a puppet – with a string running from the base of your spine to the top of your head. Imagine that the string is gently pulled upwards and your back, neck and head are perfectly aligned. Your head is at rest and comfortably settled in line with your back and spine. You are looking forward, and your head is settled in comfortably.

5. Bend your knees slightly - still standing in a comfortable position.

6. Place your hand over your stomach.

7. Take such a deep breath that you feel your stomach expand as you breathe. Follow your facilitator's instructions as you breathe deeply for a few moments.

   a. When we are stressed, we tend to take rapid shallow breaths. By learning deep breathing exercises and paying attention to what our bodies are doing, we make sure our brain is receiving enough oxygen, and we are activating the right orbital prefrontal cortex of our brain. Both of these are needed for learning.

   b. Practicing deep breathing exercises can also help us think through our options when we are distressed, and avoid making poor decisions made in hasty reactions to stress.

8. Follow your facilitator's instructions as you learn to relax your face, shoulders, arms, hands, legs, and feet. You will alternately tighten and then loosen the muscles in these areas as you follow your facilitator's directions.

   a. You may choose to remain standing, sit, or lay down on the floor during this segment of the exercise.

9. Continue to breathe deeply as your body is relaxing.

10. Return to your seats when the exercise is complete and it is time to start the Week 2 Video.

THE 2 SKILLS YOUR BRAIN CAN'T LIVE WITHOUT
THE RHYTHMS OF JOY AND QUIET

TODAY'S LESSON: The 2 Skills Your Brain Can't Live Without
The Rhythms of Joy and Quiet

CLASS NOTES: The Rhythms of Joy and Quiet

A quick review:
- Last week, we learned that we are created so that our brain functions best when it is in secure relationships.

Left and right sides of the brain
- Left Side: Naming and Explaining
- Right Side: Knowing and Experiencing

In the right brain: a four level control center
- *Level One:*
  - Attachment
  - Thalamus and basal ganglia, help regulate dopamine
- *Level Two:*
  - The guardshack: life is good, bad or scary
  - The amygdala: helps regulate adrenaline
- *Level Three:*
  - Synchronization
  - The cingulate cortex: helps regulate serotonin
  - Helps resolve negative emotions
- *Level Four:*
  - Identity
  - The right orbital prefrontal cortex
  - Helps me focus my attention, and answer the question "Who am I?"

Creation reflects rhythms of joy and quiet
- Then God said, "Let there be lights in the firmament of the heavens to divide the day from the night; and let them be for signs and seasons, and for days and years; and let them be for lights in the firmament of the heavens to give light on the earth"; and it was so….And God saw that it was good. Genesis 1: 14-15, 18. NKJV.
- We are also creatures of rhythm.

When we move easily from rhythms of joy into rhythms of quiet in relationships:
- Our brain works best.
- How do we learn the rhythms of joy and quiet?
- We learn these rhythms in relationships!

We are created for joy
- Joy is our natural state
- Joy creates our identity
- Joy is the basis for bonding
- Joy gives us our strength

THE 2 SKILLS YOUR BRAIN CAN'T LIVE WITHOUT
THE RHYTHMS OF JOY AND QUIET

Joy is why Jesus spoke to us
- "These things I have spoken to you, that my joy may be in you, and that your joy may be full." John 15:11, RSV.

How do we build joy?

Joy means relationships

Joy means: we are glad to be together. Someone is glad to be with me!

Attachment, joy and the senses: myelination of the sensory regions
- 0-6 weeks
  - Taste
  - Temperature regulation
  - Smell
- 6-12 weeks touch
- 2-12 months visual
- 12-24 months voice tone

Joy smiles synchronize mother and child from 2 – 12 months.

Right-hemisphere to right-hemisphere communication
- Right brain > left face > left side of retinas > right brain
- Six complete cycles of communication every second
- Synchronized brain chemistry
- Matched brain structure growth
- Authentic, truthful, rapid communication
- Emotions are AMPLIFIED each cycle
- Subjectively experienced as produced by the "other"

Climbing Joy Mountain: capacity
- Learning to build joy and increase capacity are tasks for the first year of life.

Before visual cortex myelination (6 weeks)
- The "dead shark" stare.
- Too young for right-hemisphere to right-hemisphere communication.
- No joy amplification yet!

3 months - visual cortex ready for joy amplification (right hemisphere)

Smile for the camera

Smile for joy

Low and high joy levels
- Can you find the baby in high joy?
- Can you find the baby in low joy?
- Who is "smiling for the camera?"

How do we learn rhythms of quiet together?

THE 2 SKILLS YOUR BRAIN CAN'T LIVE WITHOUT
THE RHYTHMS OF JOY AND QUIET

We are created for quiet together
- Quiet Together is our natural state
- Quiet Together creates our identity
- Quiet Together is the basis for bonding
- Quiet Together gives us our strength

Quiet together means:
- We are not alone.
- We can rest.
- I can still and quiet myself.
- I am undisturbed – even in the presence of my enemies, for someone is with me.

Disruption of "quiet together time" is the strongest predictor of developing a mental illness.
- SPECT Scan of a brain in depression from Dr. Daniel Amen.
- The cingulate cortex is over-active.

***Healing The Hardware of the Soul* by Dr. Daniel Amen.**
- Very practical lists and steps to help your brain work better and correct problems that produce emotional symptoms.
- Good brain scans!
- Visit www.amenclinic.com or www.brainplace.com for more information and other brain scans.

Mom and baby building joy and then sharing quiet together
- Mom and baby build joy together.
- Baby looks up and left when rest is needed.
- Mom synchronizes with baby.
- Baby and mom then share "Quiet Together"
- Field and Fogel, 1982 in "Origin of the Self" by Dr. Alan Schore, p 86.

Visual experiences and socio-emotional development
- *Unsynchronized Mother and Baby*
  - Mom is not synchronized with the baby's emotional state, and does not respond appropriately to the baby's state of emotional arousal.
  - Baby is overwhelmed.
  - There is no sharing of "Quiet Together."
- *Synchronized Mother and Baby*
  - Mom is synchronized, and responds appropriately to the baby's state of emotional arousal.
  - Baby and mom share joy together.
  - Baby and mom share "Quiet Together."
- This is from the work of Dr. Allan Schore.

We learn to synch – or sink!

Mom and baby building joy and then sharing quiet together
- "Mother Core" synchronization.
- Mom and baby synchronize and build joy together.

THE 2 SKILLS YOUR BRAIN CAN'T LIVE WITHOUT
THE RHYTHMS OF JOY AND QUIET

- Baby looks up and left when rest is needed.
- Mom would then synchronize with the baby, and they would then share "Quiet Together."
- Beebe and Lachman, 1988 in "Affect Regulation and Origin of the Self" by Dr. Allan Schore, p 81.

Photos of mom and baby sharing joy and synchronizing together
- Good mother (both low)
- Good mother (both medium)
- Just before disconnect to rest
- This is where they would share "Quiet Together" time.

We are creatures of rhythm
- Rhythmic change is our natural state.
- Rhythmic change creates our identity.
- Rhythmic change is the basis for bonding.
- Rhythmic change gives us our strength.

We learn to synch – or sink!

When our joy capacity is low, and we can't quiet ourselves, life is very painful
- We experience trauma when our level of pain exceeds our level of joy.
- Pervasive fear is pain at level 2 of the emotional control center.

Medicate to Regulate

BEEPS
- BEEPS are attachments to Behaviors, Events, Experiences, People or Substances that are used to regulate emotions, increase pleasure or decrease pain.

BEEPS
- Attachments to BEEPS help us medicate – to artificially regulate – positive and negative emotions as well as pain.

BEEPS
- Attachments to BEEPS take the place of secure attachments to God and significant others.

BEEPS
- There are many different types of BEEPS. Examples can include:
- Behaviors: Work
- Events: Thrill Seeking
- Experiences: Sex
- People: Relationships
- Substances: Alcohol

Wired to BEEPS
- Step 1: We admitted we were powerless over BEEPS - that our lives had become unmanageable.

THE 2 SKILLS YOUR BRAIN CAN'T LIVE WITHOUT
THE RHYTHMS OF JOY AND QUIET

- Using BEEPS to regulate emotions, pleasure and pain wires the brain to BEEPS.

The longer beeps are used, the stronger the connection becomes

Losing control
- Eventually, the response between unwanted emotions and pain is so strong, that the response is automatic.

BEEPS wiring leaves us powerless and life is unmanageable

Rhythms of joy and quiet rewire the brain to connect with God and others, and disconnect from BEEPS.

EXERCISE: The Mother Wound Video Discussion: *20-25 Minutes*
After watching Eileen in the "Mother Wound Video"

1. Break into groups of 3-5 people.

2. Volunteers may share answers to the following questions about the video:
   a. Did you notice a difference in Eileen's appearance between the prayer session and the follow-up?
   b. What was the difference in Eileen's life after the session with Dr. Lehman?
   c. How did you feel when you watched Eileen struggling with her decision to come to Jesus?
   d. Why was it important for Eileen to make a decision to go to Jesus? Why did Jesus wait for her to come to Him?
   e. In the video, Eileen refers to Jesus' smile. After what we've learned in this week's lesson, why is that important?
   f. What happened to Eileen's "comfort eating" and her attachment with ice cream?
   g. What do you think would happen if you could learn to experience the presence of Jesus in the painful places of your own life?

3. Your facilitator will remind you to:
   a. Stay relational by making appropriate eye contact as you share.
   b. Support each other by actively listening as others share.
   c. Please do not give advice or offer criticism or corrective comments about what others have shared.

4. Your facilitator will help you by keeping track of time.

5. Following the small group sharing, your facilitator may ask volunteers to share their insights and responses with the entire group. (Approx 10 minutes).

CLOSE THE GROUP WITH PRAYER

THE 2 SKILLS YOUR BRAIN CAN'T LIVE WITHOUT
THE RHYTHMS OF JOY AND QUIET

QUESTIONS FOR FURTHER DISCUSSION OR FOLLOW-UP

1. How do we learn the rhythms of joy and quiet?

2. Why did Jesus say that joy was important?

3. What is the primary way that moms and babies bond from 2-12 months?

4. Why is quiet together important for the brain?

5. What do rhythms of joy and quiet teach us?

6. Who built joy and quiet together time with you when you were a child?

7. How do you feel when you make eye contact with family and close friends? Why?

8. What are the messages you learned about eye contact from your family?

9. Who builds joy with you?

10. Are you able to effectively quiet and calm yourself when you are upset? What do you need to learn to more effectively quiet yourself?

11. Do you feel like your level of pain often exceeds your level of joy? How long have you felt that way? Have you felt that your level of joy was not high enough to handle the pain in your life?

12. What happens when your level of joy is overwhelmed by pain?

13. Have you ever used BEEPS to avoid feelings that you didn't like?

14. What BEEPS did you use to relieve those feelings?

15. What happens when you do not use BEEPS to medicate those feelings?

16. Have you ever decided that you didn't want to use BEEPS – but felt so overwhelmed that you used BEEPS anyway?

THE 2 SKILLS YOUR BRAIN CAN'T LIVE WITHOUT
THE RHYTHMS OF JOY AND QUIET

OPTIONAL 12 STEP QUESTIONS

1. Do you think that you've lost control of your attachments to BEEPS? Why?

2. Can you remember a time when you felt like you were able to control your use of BEEPS? Do you still feel that way now?

3. Did you ever use BEEPS when you did not plan on it? What happened?

4. Have you ever felt guilty and ashamed because of your use of BEEPS?

5. Have you ever experienced weight loss or gain that is a direct result of your use of BEEPS? Describe your experience.

6. Have BEEPS ever resulted in the loss of a relationship that was important to you? Describe your experience.

7. Have you ever spent money on BEEPS that you knew should have been spent on other people or things?
   What happened?

8. Have you ever promised others that you would cut back or stop using BEEPS? Who did you promise, and what happened? Were you able to fulfill your promise?

9. Have people close to you ever told you that they thought BEEPS were a problem for you? Who were they, and how did you respond?

10. Has your use of BEEPS ever bothered you?

11. Think about the times when you have used BEEPS. What do you usually feel like just before you use BEEPS?

12. Have you ever felt angry, sad, hopeless, afraid, disgusted or ashamed– and used BEEPS to stop the pain?

13. Have you ever used BEEPS to calm down?

14. Do you think that BEEPS help you medicate unwanted feelings?

15. Can you imagine living without BEEPS? Describe what you think your life might be like – and feel like – without BEEPS.

16. What does powerlessness mean to you?

17. What do you think you need to start dealing with the powerlessness and unmanageability that are a part of BEEPS?

RESTARTING GROUP
GROUND RULES

Wise Thoughts About Group Rules

1. You can help build joy and a recovery community for you and others. Your community thrives when you keep the personal information Restarting members share in your group confidential. Do not share it with others. Your facilitator will help you and others stay safe by reporting child or elder abuse – and any imminent danger to you or to the person or property of others.

2. Take every opportunity to build joy – and practice your joy-building skills in Restarting.

3. Express appreciation to each other frequently.

4. When you are glad to be with others, it helps them feel like they belong – and helps build a Restarting community that is joyful.

5. Supportive listening helps others share, heal and feel comfortable. It's a lot harder for others to build joy with you when you are offering criticism or advice. The directions that accompany each exercise will help you learn to offer constructive and helpful feedback that builds joy.

6. Sharing is strongly encouraged, but not required.

7. By following your facilitator's instructions and the directions in your workbook, you will help keep your group on track, learn new Restarting skills, and help provide enough time for everyone to share.

8. Encourage others to return to Restarting.

9. Following your facilitator's directions to complete all Restarting exercises in groups of 3-5 people will help you build the kind of joy that is powerful – and safe – for you and everyone else.

10. It is very difficult for you and for others to create belonging if you arrive for group intoxicated, so if you come to group "under the influence", you won't be able to participate in Restarting that evening.

11. Threats, violence and intimidation are a sign that you are overwhelmed – and are actively and intensely overwhelming others. Because these behaviors make Restarting unsafe for others, you will be unable to return to Restarting if you do them.

3 CALMING OUR PAINFUL EMOTIONS
RETURNING TO JOY, PART 1: SYNCHRONIZATION & NEGATIVE EMOTIONS

OPEN THE GROUP WITH PRAYER

YOUR NOTES

SYNCHRONIZED WALKING: *20 Minutes*

1. Your facilitator will introduce you to the concept of "synchronization," that is one of this week's topics. Synchronized walking is a good way to have fun and introduce this concept.

2. Stand up and form small groups of 3 people.

3. Follow your facilitator's instructions – as they help you and your groups line up.
   a. Each person in a group of 3 should stand side-by-side.
   b. All the small groups should form a circle around the room with plenty of space between them.

4. Your facilitator will signal the groups to start walking in a circle around the room.

5. The person in the middle of each small group walks normally. The others in their small group synchronize with the person in the middle by copying their walk and movements.

6. After the groups are synchronizing fairly well, your facilitator will let the groups know that the person in the middle of each small group can change their walk (silly walks are encouraged) and have their partners continue to synchronize with them. This can be lots of fun!

7. After 2 minutes, your facilitator will signal you that it is time to switch places. The person in the middle moves to the outside, and a new person moves into the middle. The entire exercise repeats.

8. After 2 minutes, your facilitator will signal you that it is time to switch places. The person who has not yet had a turn in the middle moves to the middle. The exercise repeats.

9. After 2 minutes, your facilitator will ask everyone to return to their seats, but remain together in groups of 3.

10. Your facilitator will ask each group to take 5 minutes and share what it felt like to synchronize together.

11. At the end of 5 minutes, your facilitator may ask volunteers to share their experience with synchronized walking with the entire group.

TODAY'S LESSON: Returning to Joy, Part One: Synchronization and Negative Emotions.

CALMING OUR PAINFUL EMOTIONS
RETURNING TO JOY, PART 1: SYNCHRONIZATION & NEGATIVE EMOTIONS

CLASS NOTES: Returning to Joy, Part 1

A quick review:
- Last week, we learned that we are created so that our brain functions best when it is in secure relationships.

Left and right sides of the brain
- Left side: naming and explaining
- Right side: knowing and experiencing

In the right brain: a four level control center
- Level One:
  - Attachment
  - Thalamus and basal ganglia, help regulate dopamine
- Level Two:
  - The guardshack: life is good, bad or scary
  - The amygdala: helps regulate adrenaline
- Level Three:
  - Synchronization
  - The cingulate cortex: helps regulate serotonin
  - Helps resolve negative emotions
- Level Four:
  - Identity
  - The right orbital prefrontal cortex
  - Helps me focus my attention, and answer the question "Who am I?"

Joy means relationships. Joy means: we are glad to be together. Someone is glad to be with me!

Right-hemisphere to right-hemisphere communication
- Right brain > left face > left side of retinas > right brain
- Six complete cycles of communication every second
- Synchronized brain chemistry
- Matched brain structure growth
- Authentic, truthful, rapid communication
- Emotions are AMPLIFIED each cycle
- Subjectively experienced as produced by the "other"

Climbing Joy Mountain - Capacity
- Learning to build joy and increase capacity are tasks for the first year of life.

We are created to flow together in rhythms of joy and quiet.

We are creatures of rhythm
- Rhythmic change is our natural state.
- Rhythmic change creates our identity.
- Rhythmic change is the basis for bonding.
- Rhythmic change gives us our strength.

CALMING OUR PAINFUL EMOTIONS
RETURNING TO JOY, PART 1: SYNCHRONIZATION & NEGATIVE EMOTIONS

We are created to be deeply connected to each other:
- In times of joy
- In quiet together
- And in the times we feel negative emotions

How do we avoid getting stuck in negative emotions, and learn to return to joy together?

We are created to be together
- Then the Lord God said, "It is not good that man should be alone. I will make him a helper fit for him." Gen 2:18, RSV.
- We are created for each other to help each other!

"Friends always show their love...What are brothers, if not to share trouble?"
- Proverbs. 17:17, Good News Bible.

Spiritual guidelines for building better brains
- Rejoice with those who rejoice
- Weep with those who weep
- Romans 12:15, RSV.

We're one but we're not the same. We get to carry each other.
- From the song "One" by U2 from the "Joshua Tree" CD.

How does our brain learn to return to joy?

Joy means relationship.

Joy means: we are glad to be together. Someone is glad to be with me!

The control center only learns "return to joy" in joyful relationships.
- It needs others to synchronize with it. **The cingulate cortex is the center for internal and external synchronization.**
- It is called "The Mother Core."
- The "Mental Banana."
- It is the center for mutual mind.

To learn to return to joy from negative emotions, I need:
- Someone with a well trained banana
  - Who knows how to return to joy from the emotion I feel
- Who is glad to be with me
  - Who has more joy than I have pain and can stay relational with me in spite of my distress
- While I am feeling the negative emotion
  - Who must synchronize with me while I am distressed

Returning to joy and quiet together is a task for the second year of life.
- When I am in distress (I experience one of the Big Six negative emotions.)
- And someone is glad to be with me. (Joy means someone is glad to be with me.)

CALMING OUR PAINFUL EMOTIONS
RETURNING TO JOY, PART 1: SYNCHRONIZATION & NEGATIVE EMOTIONS

- And shares my distress (I am able to return to joy since you are glad to be with me.)
- Now we are both feeling distressed but synchronized.
- I can start to quiet myself. (Quiet Together teaches me to quiet myself.)

I learn to self-regulate through mutual regulation
- Both are needed throughout my lifetime
- Mutual regulation is needed for:
- Learning to return to joy
- Combining joy strength

The Big Six Negative Emotions
- Anger
- Fear
- Shame
- Disgust
- Sadness
- Hopeless Despair

Pause and discuss: Why did God give us the ability to feel negative emotions?
- Anger
- Fear
- Shame
- Disgust
- Sadness
- Hopeless Despair

EXERCISE: Why Did God Give Us the Ability to Feel Negative Emotions?
25 Minutes

1. Break into small groups of at least 3 people. Your facilitator will help adjust group size depending on the total number of participants.

2. Your facilitator will assign each group one or more of the Big Six Negative Emotions. Each group will spend 10 minutes discussing the reasons why they think God has given them the ability to feel that negative emotion. One member of each group should function as a group secretary, and record everyone's input. Your facilitator will remind you when your discussion time is up.

3. After the small groups have completed their discussions, your facilitator will ask each small group to share the results of their discussions with the entire group. Your facilitator will help moderate this discussion for 10-15 minutes.

4. Following the completion of this exercise, the facilitator will restart the video.

CALMING OUR PAINFUL EMOTIONS
RETURNING TO JOY, PART 1: SYNCHRONIZATION & NEGATIVE EMOTIONS

Six basic unpleasant emotions
- Sad: I lost some of my life
- Angry: I need to protect myself and make it stop!
- Frightened: I want to "get away"
- Ashamed: I'm not bringing you joy and/or you are not glad to be with me
- Disgusted: That's not life-giving!
- Hopeless Despair: I lack the time and resources

To self-regulate, my brain must learn to return to joy from every negative emotion
- I must have connections between each negative emotion and joy

Strong connections back to joy from negative emotions must be built
- The connections back to joy from negative emotions must be strong and used frequently.

If the connections back to joy are weak or were never made at all
- For example, suppose that there are no connections back to joy from anger

I'll get stuck in anger when I feel angry
- I won't be able to stay connected to others.
- I will be consumed with trying to protect myself and make the pain stop.
- I won't act like myself

When we are unsynchronized, we get stuck in negative emotions
- Our level of pain exceeds our level of joy.
- This is experienced as trauma, and results in ongoing emotional distress.
- This is pain at Level 3 of the Control Center.

When we are unsynchronized, joy and relational capacity is low:
- Our level of pain is greater than our level of joy.
- We can't stay connected relationally with others.
- Our relationships tend to break down when we are distressed.
- Our capacity to attach to others in joyful relationships is diminished.

Medicate to regulate

Synchronized relationships increase capacity and the ability to return to joy
- Our level of joy is greater than our level of pain.
- We are able to attach securely to others.
- We have the capacity to stay relational when we are distressed.
- Joyful synchronization creates healthy attachments with God and others.

CALMING OUR PAINFUL EMOTIONS
RETURNING TO JOY, PART 1: SYNCHRONIZATION & NEGATIVE EMOTIONS

Next week: Returning To Joy, Part 2
- Synchronization and returning to joy from negative emotions.
- Satan's 2 primary strategies to keep us stuck in pain and relational breakdown.
- Introduction to capacity and attachment.
- Returning to joy, BEEPS and Step 2 of the Twelve Steps.

CLOSE THE GROUP WITH PRAYER

CALMING OUR PAINFUL EMOTIONS
RETURNING TO JOY, PART 1: SYNCHRONIZATION & NEGATIVE EMOTIONS

QUESTIONS FOR FURTHER DISCUSSION OR FOLLOW-UP

1. How did it feel trying to synchronize with others during the walking exercise? How did you feel when others were trying to synchronize with you?

2. Is it hard for you to synchronize with others?

3. Is there anyone in your life that will synchronize with you when you are upset?

4. Why did God create us to be together?

5. How does "Rejoicing with those who rejoice" and "weeping with those who weep" help the brain?

6. What are the three things you need to learn to return to joy from negative emotions?

7. Why is it important that someone else have a well-trained banana if we are going to learn to return to joy? Why is it important that they have a lot of joy strength?

8. How does staying relational help us learn to return to joy from negative emotions?

9. Do you know how to return to joy from the Big Six negative emotions? How long does it take you?

10. What negative emotions do you have the hardest time recovering from?

11. What happens to you when you get stuck in a negative emotion? What happens to your ability to stay connected to others around you?

12. Are you able to act like yourself when you experience the big six negative emotions? If not, how would you like to act when you feel one of these distressing emotions?

13. When you are experiencing one of the Big Six negative emotions, what do you want the most at that time?

14. Do you have a person with a "trained banana" in your life that can help you learn to return to joy from each one of the Big Six negative emotions?

15. Have you ever used BEEPS to medicate one of the Big Six negative emotions? What happened? Did it work?

CALMING OUR PAINFUL EMOTIONS
RETURNING TO JOY, PART 1: SYNCHRONIZATION & NEGATIVE EMOTIONS

OPTIONAL 12 STEP QUESTIONS

1. Many of us who use BEEPS are very uncomfortable with the Big Six negative emotions. Many of us use BEEPS to avoid, minimize or escape these feelings. What do you do when you feel the Big Six negative emotions?
   a. Anger
   b. Fear
   c. Sadness
   d. Shame
   e. Disgust
   f. Hopeless Despair

2. What BEEPS do you use when you feel each of these negative emotions?

3. Do BEEPS help you to return to joy from these negative emotions? What effect do BEEPS have on negative emotions in the long run?

4. Anxiety is the neurochemical equivalent of fear. We are often more aware of feeling anxious than we are of feeling afraid. Do you often feel anxious? What does your body feel like when you are anxious?

5. What happens to you when your anxiety builds? What do you feel?

6. What happens to your relationships when your anxiety grows?

7. What BEEPS do you use to relieve growing feelings of anxiety?

8. Do BEEPS make you feel less anxious?

9. What have you found that works to help you feel less anxious?

10. Have you found anything that helps you when you are experiencing a Big Six negative emotion?

11. Are you able to effectively handle negative emotions by yourself?

12. How did people in your house handle the Big Six negative emotions when you were growing up?

13. How do you feel when others around you are experiencing one of the Big Six distressing negative emotions?

14. Do you feel powerless over negative emotions?

15. Does just thinking and talking about negative emotions raise your level of anxiety?

16. Do you like how you act when you feel distressing emotions – or do you find yourself doing and saying things that you feel ashamed of later?

17. Do negative emotions make your life unmanageable?

18. What does the expression "emotionally sober" mean to you? Is it possible to be sober from the use of BEEPS – and still not be emotionally sober? Why or why not?

4 STRATEGIES THAT KEEP YOU STUCK
RETURNING TO JOY, PART 2: CAPACITY, ATTACHMENT & BEEPS

OPEN THE GROUP WITH PRAYER	YOUR NOTES

EXERCISE: THE BIG SIX EMOTIONS. *15 Minutes*

1. Break into small groups of 3 people.

2. Your facilitator will remind you of the definitions of the Big Six negative emotions from last week's lesson.   These emotions are:
   a. Sad: I lost some of my life.
   b. Angry: I need to protect myself and make it stop!
   c. Frightened: I want to "get away."
   d. Ashamed: I'm not bringing you joy and/or you are not glad to be with me.
   e. Disgusted: That's not life-giving!
   f. Hopeless Despair: I lack the time and resources.

3. Each person in the small groups will have 3 minutes to share what they learned about synchronization and the Big Six negative emotions from last week's lesson. If what you learned made a positive difference in how you handled a negative emotion in the past week, you are encouraged to share your experience.
4. Remember to stay relational as you share:
   a. Maintain appropriate eye contact.
   b. Support each other through active listening.
   c. Please do not offer criticism or advice after others have shared.

5. Your facilitator will keep track of time for you so that everyone in your group has a chance to share.

6. When this exercise is complete, your facilitator will remind you to gather into a large group for this week's lesson.

TODAY´S LESSON: Returning to Joy, Part 2
Capacity, Attachment and BEEPS

CLASS NOTES: Returning to Joy, Part 2.
Capacity, Attachment and BEEPS

A quick review:

Learning to flow together in rhythms of joy and quiet is a task for the first year of life.

STRATEGIES THAT KEEP YOU STUCK
RETURNING TO JOY, PART 2: CAPACITY, ATTACHMENT & BEEPS

Returning to joy and quiet together is a task for the second year of life.
- When I am in distress (I experience one of the Big Six negative emotions).
- And someone is glad to be with me (Joy means someone is glad to be with me).
- And shares my distress (I am able to Return to Joy since you are glad to be with me).
- Now we are both feeling distressed but synchronized.
- I can start to quiet myself (Quiet Together teaches me to quiet myself).

The control center only learns "Return to Joy" in joyful relationships
- It needs others to synchronize with it.

To learn to return to joy from negative emotions, I need:
- Someone with a well trained banana.
  - Who knows how return to joy from the emotion I feel.
- Who is glad to be with me
  - Who has more joy than I have pain and can stay relational with me in spite of my distress.
- While I am feeling the negative emotion.
  - Must synchronize with me while I am distressed.

The Big Six negative emotions
- Anger
- Fear
- Shame
- Disgust
- Sadness
- Hopeless Despair

To self-regulate, my brain must learn to return to joy from every negative emotion.
- I must have connections between each negative emotion and joy.

Strong connections back to joy from negative emotions must be built.
- The connections back to joy from negative emotions must be strong and used frequently. **If the connections back to joy are weak or were never made at all...**
- For example, suppose that there are no connections back to joy from anger.

I'll get stuck in anger when I feel angry:
- I won't be able to stay connected to others.
- I will be consumed with trying to protect myself and make the pain stop.
- I won't act like myself.

When we are unsynchronized, we get stuck in negative emotions:
- Our level of pain exceeds our level of joy.
- This is experienced as trauma, and results in ongoing emotional distress.
- This is pain at Level 3 of the Control Center.

STRATEGIES THAT KEEP YOU STUCK
RETURNING TO JOY, PART 2: CAPACITY, ATTACHMENT & BEEPS

Synchronized relationships increase capacity and the ability to return to joy:
- Our level of joy is greater than our level of pain.
- We are able to attach securely to others.
- We have the capacity to stay relational when we are distressed.
- Joyful synchronization creates healthy attachments with God and others.

When we are unsynchronized, joy and relational capacity is low:
- Our level of pain is greater than our level of joy.
- We can't stay connected relationally with others.
- Our relationships tend to break down when we are distressed.
- Our capacity to attach to others in joyful relationships is diminished.

Satan has 2 primary strategies to keep us stuck in pain and relational breakdown:
- To cause us to live our lives from pain.
- To live our lives from "The Sark."

There is one strategy for each hemisphere of the brain
- The right hemisphere
  - Pain: the pusher
- The left hemisphere
  - Sark: the picker

Pain: the pusher
- Pain in the control center means that life and relationships will be pain-driven (pushed by pain).
- Eliminating, avoiding or medicating pain becomes our most important need and motivation.
- Relationship with God is mostly about trying to eliminate, hide, avoid or medicate pain.
- Relationships with others are about avoiding, hiding or using others to relieve or medicate pain.

The sark: the picker
- The mistaken belief that we are able to pick the right and wrong course of action for our lives – one that will not hurt.
- Explanations for life, good and evil are based on the drive to eliminate, medicate or avoid pain.
- We are consumed with knowing good and evil – not God.
- It is stubborn, persistent and always wrong!

The sark is driven by the mistaken belief that it can pick the right or wrong thing to do.
- The Sark is absolutely opposed to the Spirit of God. Romans 8:6-9.

The biblically informed sark is especially problematic
- It is what crucified Jesus.

STRATEGIES THAT KEEP YOU STUCK
RETURNING TO JOY, PART 2: CAPACITY, ATTACHMENT & BEEPS

Pain and sark driven belief systems guide our understanding of good and evil.
- If it hurts, it is bad and must not be God.
- If it is less painful, it is good and must be God.
- If I serve God and it is painful:
  - It can't be God's will.
  - I must be wrong.
  - God and/or others don't care about me.
- If I serve God and it is not painful:
  - It must be God's will.
  - I must be right.
  - God and others do care.

Through pain and the sark, our capacity for joy is diminished
- Our level of pain exceeds our level of joy.
- We live in pain, feel separated from God and others and can't stay relational with them.
- These are the goals of Satan's strategies.
- We cannot securely attach to God and others in joyful relationships.

Synchronization creates capacity and attachment.

There are four types of attachments:
- Secure
- Dismissive
- Distracted
- Disorganized

BEEPS
- BEEPS are attachments to Behaviors, Events, Experiences, People or Substances that are used to regulate emotions, increase pleasure or decrease pain.

BEEPS
- Attachments to BEEPS help us medicate – to artificially regulate – positive and negative emotions as well as pain.

BEEPS
- Attachments to BEEPS take the place of secure attachments to God and significant others.

BEEPS
- There are many different types of BEEPS. Examples can include:
- Behaviors: Work
- Events: Thrill Seeking
- Experiences: Sex
- People: Relationships
- Substances: Alcohol

STRATEGIES THAT KEEP YOU STUCK
RETURNING TO JOY, PART 2: CAPACITY, ATTACHMENT & BEEPS

The Twelve Steps and return to joy
- Step 2: Came to believe that a power greater than ourselves could restore us to sanity.

BEEPS and Return to Joy:
- When we use BEEPS to avoid or regulate negative emotions, our negative emotions become wired to BEEPS.
- This means that negative emotions will powerfully trigger the drive to use BEEPS.
- It becomes almost impossible to avoid BEEPS when triggered.

This wiring between negative emotions and BEEPS are part of the insanity of BEEPS:
- We do the same things, over and over again, and expect different results.
- But because our wiring doesn't change, we are triggered by the same feelings and get the same result: BEEPS!

When we feel a negative emotion like hopeless despair:
- We use BEEPS to medicate it, until we don't feel distressed, or the level of pleasure from BEEPS covers our level of pain.

We need a power greater than ourselves who can restore us to sanity…
- We need God – and others:
  - With well trained brains
  - Who are empowered by joy
  - Who know how to handle the emotion
  - Who are glad to be with us in our distress

That's how we learn to return to joy and stay relational with each other!

LEARNING TO TELL LEVEL 4+ JOY STORIES

These materials are from:
- "The Life Model: Living from the Heart Jesus Gave You." By Dr. E. James Wilder and others.
- Level 4+ slides are from "THRIVE Sensible Strategies" by Chris and Jen Coursey, © 2006.

Level 4+ Stories:
- Include both the left and right hemispheres of the brain
- Provide examples of how we are to act when upset
- Give us practice – the more we tell, the better we become
- Help us use words for emotions and body sensations
- Give us opportunity to gather emotion stories for use at other times with other people
- Give us opportunity to critique others' stories and receive feedback. This improves mind sight

STRATEGIES THAT KEEP YOU STUCK
RETURNING TO JOY, PART 2: CAPACITY, ATTACHMENT & BEEPS

- Build our capacity to return to joy from distress and increase our ability to regulate our own emotions
- Illustrate how others act like themselves
- Spark memories to find our own stories
- Build bonds and create a group identity

Characteristics of Level 4+ stories
- Describe what your body feels during the emotions
- It must be a story you have told before
- Use enough words to describe what is occurring from your point of view
  Let the listeners into "your world" descriptively
- Use feeling words to describe body sensations
- Make it autobiographical; you are involved
- State specifically how you like to act during the emotion
- Maintain eye contact (stay relational) during the story telling

Level 4+ story Guidelines
- Pick a story you do not need to be guarded in telling
- The story must illustrate and evoke the feeling
- Show the authentic emotion in your voice and face
- Do not pick an intense story – rather, find one with a medium feeling level

4+ Synchronized story Summary
- Use enough words for others to understand easily
- Use feeling words for sensations and emotions
- Be autobiographical; you are involved
- Maintain eye contact during story telling
- Stay relational
- Show authentic emotions on your face and in your voice
- Describe how your body feels during the emotions
- Tell specifically how you like to act during the emotions

Preparing My Level 4+ Story Worksheet

1. This story has a moderate feeling level and is not too intense

2. I have told this story before

3. I do not need to be guarded in telling this story

4. This story is autobiographical (I am involved in the story)

5. This story illustrates a specific feeling

6. I will show the authentic emotion on my face and in my voice

7. I will maintain eye contact while storytelling

8. Briefly describe the situation:

9. Feeling words for this story:

STRATEGIES THAT KEEP YOU STUCK
RETURNING TO JOY, PART 2: CAPACITY, ATTACHMENT & BEEPS

10. During this story my body felt:

11. The things I did in this story that demonstrate how I like to act in this emotion are (or if I did not act like myself at the time, it would have been like me to do this...)

Follow your level 4+ story worksheet as you listen Ed's Level 4+ Joy Story.

Tell a Level 4+ Joy Story!

EXERCISE: LEARNING TO TELL A LEVEL 4+ JOY STORY *30 Minutes*

1. Break into small groups of 3 people.

2. Take 5 minutes to complete the "Preparing My 4+ Story Worksheet" that is in your workbook. Your facilitator will review the worksheet with you and may use Ed's Level 4+ Joy Story from the video to help you recognize the elements and characteristics of a Level 4+ story.

   a. Please make sure that your story is not so emotionally intense that it overwhelms others.

   b. It helps if this is a story that you have told before – this makes it easier to share.

   c. It is a good idea to avoid stories that may cause you or others feelings of shame or embarrassment.

   d. Make sure that the story is about your feelings and that you are involved in the story.

   e. Be sure that your story clearly illustrates a specific feeling.

   f. As you tell your story, let your face and voice reflect the emotion you are describing.

   g. As you maintain eye contact with others in your small group, it will help you stay connected relationally with them.

   h. Write a brief description of the situation you want to share. You only need to write down enough details to help you remember the story – and be able to share it.

   i. Write the feeling words that describe the emotions that you felt during the story. It helps to list each one.

   j. Write down how your body felt during the situation you are describing. It may be things like: "my stomach was in a knot" or "my shoulders felt tight" or "my muscles felt relaxed."

   k. Describe what you did in the situation that illustrates how you like to act when you are feeling that specific emotion. What is it like you to do when you are feeling great joy? Maybe you like to tell others how excited you feel – or perhaps you like to say a quick "thanks" to God. If you didn't act like yourself when you had the feeling you are describing, what would it have been like you to do?

STRATEGIES THAT KEEP YOU STUCK
RETURNING TO JOY, PART 2: CAPACITY, ATTACHMENT & BEEPS

EXERCISE: LEARNING TO TELL A LEVEL 4+ JOY STORY *Continued*

3. Your facilitator will tell a Level 4+ Joy Story.

4. Your facilitator will ask you for feedback that describes how well their Level 4+ story met the guidelines listed on your worksheet.
   a. Locate the guidelines for Level 4+ stories on your worksheet.
   b. Your facilitator will read the first characteristic of a Level 4+ story.
   c. Your facilitator will ask you if the story met that guideline, and listen to your feedback.
   d. Your facilitator will repeat this process until they have received feedback based on every Level 4+ story characteristic.

5. Take 5 minutes and complete the worksheet for your own Level 4+ story. Your facilitator will help you by keeping track of time.

6. Your facilitator will ask for volunteers in each small group to begin telling a Level 4+ Joy Story. You will have 3 minutes to tell your story. Your facilitator will keep track of time for you. If at any point your group gets stuck or has a question, please raise your hand, and your facilitator will come help you.

7. After the first joy story, each group can take 2 minutes to give feedback on the story. Use the "Preparing My 4+ Story Worksheet" as a guideline to help the story teller discover if they were able to share all the elements of a 4+ story that are listed on the worksheet. Be encouraging and positive! Your facilitator will keep track of time for you, and let you know when it is time for the next person to share their story.

8. Your facilitator will let you know when it is time for a second person in each small group to begin their 3-minute Level 4+ Joy Story, followed by 2 minutes of feedback. Your facilitator will keep track of time for you and let you know when it is time for the next person to share their story.

9. Your facilitator will let you know when it is time for the third person in each small group to begin their 3-minute Level 4+ Joy Story, followed by 2 minutes of feedback. Your facilitator will keep track of time for you.

10. At the conclusion of the exercise, your facilitator may ask volunteers to share about their experience with the entire group. Use one word to describe how it felt to share and hear joy stories.

CLOSE THE GROUP WITH PRAYER

PREPARING MY 4+ JOY STORY WORKSHEET

1. This story has a moderate feeling level and is not too intense ☐

2. I have told this story before ☐

3. I do not need to be guarded in telling this story ☐

4. This story is autobiographical (I am involved in the story) ☐

5. This story illustrates a specific feeling ☐

6. I will show the authentic emotion on my face and in my voice ☐

7. I will maintain eye contact while storytelling ☐

8. Briefly describe the situation:

9. Feeling words for this story:

10. During this story my body felt:

11. The things I did in this story that demonstrate how I like to act in this emotion are (or if I did not act like myself at the time, it would have been like me to do this...)

STRATEGIES THAT KEEP YOU STUCK
RETURNING TO JOY, PART 2: CAPACITY, ATTACHMENT & BEEPS

QUESTIONS FOR FURTHER DISCUSSION OR FOLLOW-UP

1. Have you noticed a difference in how you think about or deal with negative emotions in the past week?
   What if anything is different?

2. Can you imagine what it would be like to stay connected to others when you experience a negative emotion?
   How would you act? What would it feel like?

3. What are Satan's two primary strategies to keep us stuck in pain and relational breakdown?

4. When you are stuck in pain, what do you spend most of your time trying to do? How does this affect you – and your relationships?

5. Is your relationship with God different when you are feeling a lot of pain? How does it change?

6. What does living in pain "push" you to do?

7. How do you define "The Sark?"

8. What is it about your own sark that keeps you stuck? How does your sark affect you?

9. Are you able to pick the right thing or wrong thing to do in your life? Why?

10. Why is it so hard to realize that our sark is always wrong?

11. What belief systems in your life are pain and sark driven? How do these keep you stuck?

12. What are the four attachment styles? Briefly describe each one.

13. What does Step 2 mean to you? Describe it in your own words.

14. Why do we need to be restored to sanity when we use BEEPS to regulate negative emotions?

15. Has the statement been true in your life? "We use BEEPS to medicate until we don't feel distressed or the level of pleasure from BEEPS covers our level of pain." Explain.

16. What do we need to be restored to sanity?

17. Can you break the strength of BEEPS attachments by sheer willpower? Why or why not?

18. Do you think that learning to tell Level 4+ Joy Stories can help increase your joy capacity? Explain.

STRATEGIES THAT KEEP YOU STUCK
RETURNING TO JOY, PART 2: CAPACITY, ATTACHMENT & BEEPS

OPTIONAL 12 STEP QUESTIONS

1. What is Step 2? Describe it in your own words.

2. Insanity has been described as "Doing the same thing, over and over again, and expecting a different result."
   Has this been true of your relationship with BEEPS?

3. Can you remember a time when you decided that you wanted to stop using a BEEPS – and really meant it – only to find that you used BEEPS again anyway? Describe this event.
   a. What BEEPS were you using?
   b. Why did you decide to stop using? What happened to cause you to make this decision?
   c. What actions did you take to stop using?
   d. What happened just before you used again?
   e. What emotions were you feeling just before you used again?
   f. What was your body feeling just before you used again?
   g. What happened when you used BEEPS again?
   h. What emotions did you feel afterwards – and in the next few days?
   i. How many times did you repeat this cycle?

4. Have you ever used more than one BEEPS to help medicate your feelings?

5. Have you ever stopped using one BEEPS, and then started or increased the use of another? Did this solve anything?

6. What has happened to relationships that are important to you when you tried to stop using BEEPS, and relapsed back into them? List each relationship that was affected.

7. What happens to your feelings about yourself when you try to stop using BEEPS – and can't?

8. Have you ever asked God to help you stop BEEPS? What happened?

9. Did you ever feel angry or disappointed with God after you asked Him for help – and then used again later?

10. Are you capable of changing the wiring between BEEPS and negative emotions in your brain?

11. Do you have specific negative emotions that are wired to BEEPS? What are they?

12. Have you ever tried to avoid specific negative emotions so that you would not use BEEPS? Have you been able to successfully avoid them? List each emotion you've tried to avoid – and your strategy for avoiding each.

13. Has your willpower alone been enough to change your attachments with BEEPS? Why?

14. What do you need to be restored back to sanity? Be specific.

15. Where can you go to find this help?

PREPARING MY 4+ JOY STORY WORKSHEET

1. This story has a moderate feeling level and is not too intense ☐

2. I have told this story before ☐

3. I do not need to be guarded in telling this story ☐

4. This story is autobiographical (I am involved in the story) ☐

5. This story illustrates a specific feeling ☐

6. I will show the authentic emotion on my face and in my voice ☐

7. I will maintain eye contact while storytelling ☐

8. Briefly describe the situation:

9. Feeling words for this story:

10. During this story my body felt:

11. The things I did in this story that demonstrate how I like to act in this emotion are (or if I did not act like myself at the time, it would have been like me to do this...)

5 HEALTHY RELATIONSHIPS
WHAT IS SECURE ATTACHMENT?

OPEN THE GROUP WITH PRAYER

EXERCISE: A LEVEL 4+ JOY STORY *15 Minutes*

1. The facilitator will ask two volunteers to share a Level 4+ Joy Story with the entire group.

2. Due to time constraints, volunteers are encouraged to share their joy story from last week.

3. Be sure to stay relational while telling the story.

4. Each story should be limited to 3 minutes. Your facilitator will help you keep track of time.

5. After each story, the facilitator and group will have the opportunity to give feedback. Use the "Preparing My 4+ Story Worksheet" as a guideline to help the storyteller discover if he/she was able to share all the elements of a 4+ story listed on the worksheet. Be encouraging and positive! Feedback should last for 2 minutes, and your facilitator will keep track of time for you.

TODAY´S LESSON: What is a Secure Attachment?

CLASS NOTES: What is a Secure Attachment?

When attachment is secure, life is powered by joy.
- We can synchronize with each other.
- We can bond and work together in joy.
- We fulfill our purpose and destiny together!

God created us to securely attach to Him and each other in joy!

We are created for relationship with God.
- Then God said, "Let Us make man in Our image, according to Our likeness… So God created man in His own image; in the image of God He created him; male and female He created them. Then God saw everything that He had made, and indeed it was very good. Genesis 1:26, 27, 31. NKJV
- God worked with Adam to name animals. Genesis 2:7.
- God walked with Adam and Eve in the cool part of the day. Genesis 3:8.

HEALTHY RELATIONSHIPS
WHAT IS SECURE ATTACHMENT ?

Even if we're stuck in negative emotions, or don't feel good enough to attach to Him, or struggle with things we feel ashamed of, God is totally committed to joyful relationship with us.

Jesus said:
- "Behold, I stand at the door and knock. If anyone hears My voice and opens the door, I will come in to him and dine with him, and he with Me."

Revelation 3:20 NKJV.

We are also created for secure attachment to each other.
- …And the Lord God said, "It is not good that man should be alone; I will make him a helper comparable to him…He brought her to the man. And Adam said: "This is now bone of my bones and flesh of my flesh…Therefore a man shall leave his father and mother and be joined to his wife, and they shall become one flesh." And they were both naked, the man and his wife, and were not ashamed.

Genesis 2:18, 23-25, NKJV.

Secure attachment means:
- Adam and Eve experienced joyful relationship with God and each other.
- They were synchronized together in rhythms of joy and quiet together.
- Securely bonded intimately for life.
- They could fulfill their purpose and destiny together.

Why do we need secure attachment to be fulfilled?
- What did God create us to do?

Be fruitful and multiply
- Bring and give life wherever you go.

Subdue, have dominion, rule
- Take relationships and Eden to places they've never been.

Serve, steward and work
- Maintain and guard what we've been given.

Protect, serve and enjoy family as mature parents
- Pass on to the next generation what I've been given.

Experience and enjoy pleasure together
- The word "Eden" means "Pleasure."

Learn truth in joyful relationships
- Know God and each other – not good and evil.

Choose who we will serve
- God, each other – or ourselves.

HEALTHY RELATIONSHIPS
WHAT IS SECURE ATTACHMENT ?

We are created with each of these desires, drives and purposes
- And we are designed to be completely fulfilled only in joyful, secure relationships with God and each other.

What happens when we are not securely attached?
- What is attachment pain?

Attachment pain is distress at level 1 of the emotional control center in the right hemisphere of the brain.
- It is the deepest level of pain.

Level 1 attachment pain:
- Attachment pain is the deepest level of pain.
- It is sub-cortical – below our conscious awareness.
- It results from insecure or disorganized attachments.
- It is what we feel when we don't know where we belong or have someone to belong to.
- It is what we feel when we don't know who and what is personal to me.
- It pervades and affects every area of life.
- Everything hurts!

EXERCISE: ATTACHMENT PAIN AND POPULAR MUSIC *5 Minutes*

1. Because attachment pain is sub-cortical, it is below our level of conscious awareness, and is often very difficult to recognize. This exercise is a fun way to learn to identify and describe attachment pain – and what it feels like.

2. Your facilitator will begin by sharing a few of his/her favorite songs with a theme of attachment pain with the entire group.

3. Volunteers can then take turns sharing their favorite attachment pain songs and lyrics with the entire group. This can be a lot of fun – and singing is not required! What songs about attachment pain do you know, and what stories do they tell?

4. Your facilitator will help you keep track of time, and will turn the DVD back on when the exercise is complete.

Attachment pain
- If joy is shared, attachment grows even when you planned and agreed not to do so.
- Makes good solutions turn sour or sexual.
- Adds intensity to everything at higher levels and should be suspected when solutions to obvious higher level problems do not work.
- Drives cutting and other addictions like food.

HEALTHY RELATIONSHIPS
WHAT IS SECURE ATTACHMENT ?

EXERCISE: HOW BADLY DOES ATTACHMENT PAIN HURT? *5 Minutes*

1. Because attachment pain is below our conscious level of aware-ness, it is often very difficult to describe what it feels like. Some-times, we don't even have words to describe that level of pain. This exercise can help us learn new feeling words that can help us describe and better understand attachment pain.

2. Your facilitator will start by giving a few one or two word examples that describe how attachment pain feels. Your facilitator may also share:
   a. His/her own feelings of attachment pain
   b. Feelings of attachment pain described in the songs from the pre-vious exercise

3. Your facilitator will ask volunteers to share one or two word de-scriptions that illustrate the feeling of attachment pain. Please limit your responses to one or two words only. This will help everyone from being overwhelmed by overly intense descriptions of attach-ment pain.

4. Your facilitator will help you keep track of time, and will turn the DVD back on when the exercise is complete.

Unrecognized attachment pain
- Recognition and interpretation are learned.
- Addictions and the nucleus accumbens.
- Masturbation.
- Quick fixes and "miracle" breakthroughs are seen as the way out. Long-term healing relationships with God and others are seen as unnecessary, unimportant or "unspiritual."
- Rescuing and over-involvement.
- Mistaken attempts at "therapeutic parenting" because attachment pain – not the needs of the child – drive it.

EXERCISE: CAN ATTACHMENT PAIN LEAD TO BEEPS? *5 Minutes*

1. Attachment pain frequently is the unrecognized pain that drives attachments to BEEPS. This exercise can help you recognize the connections between attachment pain and BEEPS. You do not need to tell a Level 4+ story in this exercise.

HEALTHY RELATIONSHIPS
WHAT IS SECURE ATTACHMENT ?

2. Your facilitator will give you a few examples of the connection between attachment pain and BEEPS. Your facilitator may:

   a. Share about a time in which he/she felt attachment pain and used BEEPS to medicate it. He/she will use a few words to describe their attachment pain, and then what BEEPS he/she used.

   b. Share a few examples of songs that illustrate the connection between attachment pain and BEEPS.

3. Your facilitator will ask volunteers to share any songs they know that illustrate the connections between attachment pain and BEEPS.

4. Your facilitator may ask if anyone in the group has ever used BEEPS to medicate attachment pain.

   a. You may respond to this question only if you feel comfortable doing so.

   b. Volunteers may answer "yes" by raising their hands.

5. Your facilitator will help you keep track of time, and will turn the DVD back on when the exercise is complete.

We are created to attach to God and others.
- If attachment is broken – or not secure, we will attach to someone or something to make the pain stop.

Medicate to regulate

BEEPS
- BEEPS are attachments to Behaviors, Events, Experiences, People or Substances that are used to regulate emotions, increase pleasure or decrease pain.

BEEPS
- Attachments to BEEPS help us medicate – to artificially regulate – positive and negative emotions as well as pain.

BEEPS
- Attachments to BEEPS take the place of secure attachments to God and significant others.

BEEPS
- There are many different types of BEEPS. Examples can include:
- Behaviors: Work
- Events: Thrill Seeking
- Experiences: Sex
- People: Relationships
- Substances: Alcohol

HEALTHY RELATIONSHIPS
WHAT IS SECURE ATTACHMENT ?

BEEPS and attachment pain bring us:
- Absolute powerlessness
  - We are incapable of fixing the problem. It is simply too big.
- Absolute unmanageability
  - No matter how hard we try, our lives are totally out of control.
- Absolute insanity
  - Our emotions and logic are hopelessly distorted. We live in pain – but deny the reality of the problem – and blame everyone but BEEPS!

Secure attachment and the Twelve Steps
- Step 3: Made a decision to turn our will and our lives over to the care of God as we understood Him.

When I turn my will and life over to the care of Jesus:
- He attaches to me in absolute and complete joy.
- My life will not be the same!

EXERCISE: TELL A LEVEL 4+ STORY ABOUT SECURE ATTACHMENT
35 Minutes

1. This exercise will help you learn to tell a Level 4+ story about secure attachment.

2. Locate your Level 4+ Secure Attachment Story Worksheet that is in your workbook. Your facilitator will take 5 minutes to review the worksheet and characteristics of a Level 4+ story with you.

3. To help you begin thinking about secure attachment, your facilitator will ask the question, "What do secure attachments feel like?"
   a. Your facilitator will share a few words describing what secure attachments with God and others feel like to him/her.
   b. Your facilitator will ask volunteers to share one word describing what secure attachments with God and others feel like.
   c. You will have 3 minutes for this part of the exercise, and your facilitator will keep track of time for you.

4. Your facilitator will share a Level 4+ Secure Attachment Story with you. After the story, your facilitator will ask the group for feedback. Did his/her story include all the characteristics listed on the worksheet? You will have 5 minutes for this part of the exercise. Your facilitator will keep track of time for you.

5. Break into groups of 3 people.

6. Take 5 minutes to complete the "Preparing My Level 4+ Secure Attachment Story" worksheet that is in your workbook. For this exercise:
   a. If you have ever had a relationship with a person who has a se-

HEALTHY RELATIONSHIPS
WHAT IS SECURE ATTACHMENT ?

cure attachment style, describe a specific experience that you had with them.

b. If you have never had a relationship with a person who has a secure attachment style, you may describe a time in which you experienced secure attachment in your relationship with God.

c. If you have had no experience with secure attachments, imagine what a secure attachment might feel like. Complete your worksheet, and describe what kind of securely attached relationship you would like to have. How do you think it might feel? How do you think you would like to act in a secure relationship? Have you ever seen a securely attached relationship between others?

d. Your facilitator will help you know when it is time to begin telling stories.

7. Your facilitator will ask for volunteers in each small group to begin telling a Level 4+ Secure Attachment Story. You will have 3 minutes to tell your story. Your facilitator will keep track of time for you. If at any point your group is stuck or has a question, please raise your hand, and your facilitator will come help you.

8. After the first secure attachment story, each group can take 2 minutes to give feedback on the story. Use the "Preparing My Level 4+ Secure Attachment Story" worksheet as a guideline to help the storyteller discover if he/she was able to share all the elements of a 4+ story that are listed on the worksheet. Be encouraging and positive! Your facilitator will keep track of time for you, and let you know when it is time for the next person to share his/her story.

9. Your facilitator will let you know when it is time for a second person in each small group to begin his/her 3-minute Level 4+ Secure Attachment Story, followed by 2 minutes of feedback. Your facilitator will keep track of time for you and let you know when it is time for the next person to share his/her story.

10. Your facilitator will let you know when it is time for the third person in each small group to begin his/her 3-minute Level 4+ Secure Attachment Story, followed by 2 minutes of feedback. Your facilitator will keep track of time for you.

11. At the conclusion of the exercise, participants may remain in their small groups. If time permits, your facilitator will ask volunteers to share about their experiences with the entire group. Use one word to describe how it felt to share and hear stories about secure attachment.

CLOSE THE GROUP WITH PRAYER

PREPARING MY 4+ SECURE ATTACHMENT STORY WORKSHEET

1. This story has a moderate feeling level and is not too intense ☐

2. I have told this story before ☐

3. I do not need to be guarded in telling this story ☐

4. This story is autobiographical (I am involved in the story) ☐

5. This story illustrates a specific feeling ☐

6. I will show the authentic emotion on my face and in my voice ☐

7. I will maintain eye contact while storytelling ☐

8. Briefly describe the situation:

9. Feeling words for this story:

10. During this story my body felt:

11. The things I did in this story that demonstrate how I like to act in this emotion are (or if I did not act like myself at the time, it would have been like me to do this...)

HEALTHY RELATIONSHIPS
WHAT IS SECURE ATTACHMENT ?

QUESTIONS FOR FURTHER DISCUSSION OR FOLLOW-UP

1. What does "secure attachment" mean to you?

2. Do you think that anything you have done keeps God from wanting a secure attachment with you? Why?

3. Have you ever avoided God because you felt ashamed of BEEPS – or didn't feel "good enough" to attach to Him? What made you feel this way?

4. Have you ever felt like you had to "clean up" or "behave" so that God would be happy to be with you? What did you do to try to improve yourself? Did it work?

5. What does Revelation 3:20 mean to you?

6. Why do you need a secure attachment to be fulfilled?

7. What do you think life would be like if you could bring and give life wherever you go?

8. How would you describe attachment pain? What is it?

9. Why does attachment pain make good solutions turn sour or sexual? Has this ever happened to you?

10. Why is it important for you to learn to recognize attachment pain?

11. Have you ever tried a "quick fix" for attachment pain? Describe the pain – and what happened when you tried the "quick fix."

12. Have you ever tried to use God or a religious experience as a "quick fix" for attachment pain? What happened?

13. What BEEPS have you used to medicate or relieve attachment pain? Use the list below to mark the BEEPS that you've used in attachment pain. Did any of these work?

- ☐ Alcohol
- ☐ Other Drugs
- ☐ Relationships
- ☐ Sex
- ☐ Food
- ☐ Gambling
- ☐ Work
- ☐ Performance/Perfectionism
- ☐ Thrill-seeking Behaviors
- ☐ Computer
- ☐ Video Games
- ☐ TV
- ☐ Money
- ☐ Power and Control
- ☐ Internet or Internet Pornography
- ☐ Religion or Ministry
- ☐ Cutting
- ☐ Rage
- ☐ Other: Be Specific

HEALTHY RELATIONSHIPS
WHAT IS SECURE ATTACHMENT ?

QUESTIONS FOR FURTHER DISCUSSION OR FOLLOW-UP

14. Have BEEPS brought you to a place of absolute powerlessness, absolute unmanageability and absolute insanity? Why – or why not?

15. What does it mean to "turn your will and life" over to the care of God?

16. Who is God – and who do you understand God to be? Draw a picture illustrating your concept of God – and your relationship to Him.

17. What did you learn from the Level 4+ secure attachment stories?

OPTIONAL 12-STEP QUESTIONS

1. What BEEPS have you used to medicate or relieve attachment pain? Use the list below to mark the BEEPS that you've used in attachment pain. Did any of these work?

☐ Alcohol
☐ Other Drugs
☐ Relationships
☐ Sex
☐ Food
☐ Gambling
☐ Work
☐ Performance/Perfectionism
☐ Thrill-seeking Behaviors
☐ Computer
☐ Video Games
☐ TV
☐ Money
☐ Power and Control
☐ Internet or Internet Pornography
☐ Religion or Ministry
☐ Cutting
☐ Rage
☐ Other: Be Specific

2. Does attachment pain make your life unmanageable? Does it leave you feeling powerless?

3. Insanity can be described as "doing the same thing over and over again, and always expecting a different result. Does medicating attachment pain with BEEPS fit this definition of insanity?

4. What is Step 3? Describe it in your own words.

5. What does it mean to turn your will over to the care of God? What does it mean to you?

6. What does it mean to turn your life over to the care of God? What does it mean to you?

7. What did you learn and believe about God growing up?

HEALTHY RELATIONSHIPS
WHAT IS SECURE ATTACHMENT ?

OPTIONAL 12-STEP QUESTIONS

8. Who had the most influence on your concept of God when you were a child? Was there a difference between what they said about God – and how they lived? How did this affect you?

9. What did your concept of God look like when you were a child? What kind of attachment did you have with Him? Draw a picture that illustrates your concept of God at that time in your life – and your attachment with Him.

10. What kind of choices did you make about your attachment with God when you were old enough to make them for yourself?

11. Has your use of BEEPS ever affected your attachment with God? Draw a picture that illustrates how BEEPS have affected this relationship.

12. What do you believe about God at this point in your life? What do you think God is like? What kind of relationship would you like to have with God now?

13. What is your attachment with God at this time? Draw a picture that illustrates your attachment with Him at this point in your life.

14. Do you think God cares about your life? How would you like Him to help you?

15. What do you believe about Jesus? Do you think that He is willing to help you if you ask?

16. Are you afraid that you will be disappointed if you ask Jesus to help you?

17. Is there anybody in your life that could help you grow in your understanding of God? Who are they? Are you willing to ask them to help you?

18. Making a decision is a very left-brained logical process. Attachment is a right brain process that involves relationship and experience with the person we want to attach to.
    a. What do you think would happen if you asked Jesus if He was willing to help you? Would you like to ask Him for help?
    b. Take a moment and ask Him this question, "Jesus, are you willing to help me?"
    c. Wait quietly for a few minutes, and pay attention to any impression, experience or perception that you may have.
    d. Write down any impression, experience or perceptions that you may have.
    e. Ask the person that you've identified in question 17 to help you understand this experience.

WHAT COMES NEXT?
RESTARTING

Your second 90 days

When you have completed Restarting in your first 90 days, you are ready for the next module in the Thriving: Recover Your Life Program, which is called Belonging. In Belonging, you will be able to spend 3 months continuing to build joy and growing in recovery and relationship skills. Belonging is training for your brain's control system. You will learn:

- How can I create a place for others to belong in joy around me…and develop life-giving relationships?

- How do I experience appreciation and self-quieting.

- What keeps me alone – and keeps me from creating a place for others to belong with me?

- How can I keep the relational part of my brain working so that I am able to actually connect with God and others.

- How can I practically restore my relational circuits if they are not working well?

- Why do people like – or hate – me, and what can I do about it?

- How do I recognize and deal with the pain that makes me relapse into addictive or abuse driven behaviors…before I relapse?

- What are the skills I need to make my cravings stop in their tracks?

- How can I see my life and others like God does?

- What do I do when I feel overwhelmed by others so that I calm down quickly?

- How can I learn to respond well to others…and not overwhelm or ignore them?

Your third 90 days

Your third 90 days you will be spend in the Healing module. You need time to learn to heal. This training helps you experience the presence of God in a way that helps you heal from the devastating effects of addictions, trauma, neglect and abuse. In Healing, you will work in small groups to continue to learn and practice the Immanuel Process. You will discover:

- How can I connect with God to talk with Him about my pain?

- How can unhappy memories silently block my awareness of God?

- What steps can I take to resolve these problems?

- Why does God want to connect with me anyway?

- What can I do when I get stuck working through something painful in my life?

- How can I learn to help others begin to talk with God about their pain?

- How can I learn to have a more stable identity, even when things are going wrong?

- How can we as a group all heal, grow and move forward in joy together?

Finishing your first year in recovery – the last 90 days

The Loving module will help you to apply practically all you have learned in the Thriving Program. Your focus is growing relationships with the people in your life that you care about the most. You will work on the skills needed to:

- Build relationships that help my recovery.

- Remove the fear that keeps me from relating to those closest to me.

- Create a place for those I care about to belong with me in joy.

- Know how attachment pain has kept me from relating to those I care about.

- Know what do when relationships don't heal.

- Continue to connect with God to resolve ongoing pain in my relationships.

6 PAINFUL RELATIONSHIPS
DISMISSIVE AND DISTRACTED ATTACHMENT

| OPEN THE GROUP WITH PRAYER | YOUR NOTES |

EXERCISE: ATTACHMENT PAIN SONGS *5 Minutes*

1. This exercise helps review the concept of attachment pain as it is expressed in popular music. In this exercise, your group will vote to determine its favorite attachment pain song.

2. Your facilitator will share one or two songs with a theme of attachment pain.

3. Your facilitator will ask volunteers to share about an attachment pain song they heard in the past week – or one they have thought about since the last session.

4. Ask the group to pay attention to the songs that volunteers share.

5. When the last volunteer has shared, the group can vote (raise their hands) to decide which song best describes attachment pain.

TODAY'S LESSON: Dismissive and Distracted Attachment

CLASS NOTES: Dismissive and Distracted Attachment

There are four attachment styles
- Secure
- Dismissive
- Distracted
- Disorganized

Secure attachment results from high joy capacity and synchronized bonds.
- How do non-secure attachments form?

Non-secure attachments result from:
- Lack of joy capacity.
- Lack of synchronization.
- Getting stuck in pain without the ability to return to joy.
- These keep us further disconnected from joyful relationships with God and others.

What happened to separate us?
- Even when we want our relationships to work?
- Why do relationships hurt so much?

PAINFUL RELATIONSHIPS
DISMISSIVE AND DISTRACTED ATTACHMENT

After the Fall:

- Then the eyes of both of them were opened, and they knew that they were naked; and they sewed fig leaves together and made themselves coverings. And they heard the sound of the Lord God walking in the garden in the cool of the day, and Adam and his wife hid themselves from the presence of the Lord God among the trees of the garden. Then the Lord God called to Adam and said to him, "Where are you?" So he said, "I heard Your voice in the garden, and I was afraid because I was naked; and I hid myself." And He said, "Who told you that you were naked? Have you eaten from the tree of which I commanded you that you should not eat?" Then the man said, "The woman whom You gave to be with me, she gave me of the tree, and I ate." And the Lord God said to the woman, "What is this you have done?" The woman said, "The serpent deceived me, and I ate."

    Genesis 3:7-10. NKJV.

Fear

Shame

Covering up

Hiding and denial

Blaming and accusing

Anger

- To Adam he said, "Cursed is the ground because of you; through painful toil you will eat of it all the days of your life. It will produce thorns and thistles for you, and you will eat the plants of the field. By the sweat of your brow (your sweaty, angry, red face) you will eat your food until you return to the ground, since from dust you were taken; for dust you are and to dust you will return.

    Gen. 3:17-19, NIV, (parenthesis and highlight added).

Sadness

- To the Woman he said, "I will greatly increase your pains (sorrows) in childbearing; with pain you will give birth to children. Your desire will be for your husband, and he will rule over you.

    Gen. 3:16 NIV, (parenthesis and highlight added).

Relationships – that were designed to be a source of strength and joy – became a source of pain.

- Lack of synchronization, diminished capacity and pain drive insecure attachments.

Non-secure attachments can lead to pain at any level of the control center.

- Level 1: Attachment pain
- Level 2: Pervasive fear
- Level 3: Desynchronized, stuck in negative emotions

PAINFUL RELATIONSHIPS
DISMISSIVE AND DISTRACTED ATTACHMENT

- Level 4: Immaturity
- Level 5: Inconsistent identity

Dismissive attachment

Dismissive
- Parent/caregiver not available.
- Detached and not synchronized to child needs for attachment on a regular basis.
- I can't expect connection, so I will live life on my own.
- Low affect, rejection, anger.
- Virtual Other: uncaring, unavailable.

Attachment light: Off
- The control center is underdeveloped.
- Life is painful – but less painful than having no one to attach to me.
- It is stuck in a parasympathetic dominant state of response to people and relationships.
- Copes through energy-conservation state of withdrawal.
- Has problems shifting out of low arousal states into intense negative or positive affect.

Adult relationships:
- Distant and avoidant.
- Withdrawal as coping strategy.
- May be highly competent or workaholic – but will operate from duty – not joy.
- Can't synchronize or share mutual mind.
- Dismisses the importance of emotions and relationships.
- Life is safer – and feels better alone and undisturbed.

What does dismissive attachment look like?
- Pause for a Level 4 Dismissive Attachment Story

EXERCISE: TELLING A LEVEL 4 DISMISSIVE ATTACHMENT STORY
10 Minutes.

1. For this exercise, it is not necessary to break into small groups.

2. Your facilitator will explain Level 4 stories.
   a. Level 4 stories are non-verbal stories that are told without using words.
   b. Level 4+ stories combine elements of both the left hemisphere (words) and right hemisphere (emotions) of the brain.
   c. Level 4 stories express the experiences, feelings, and sensations of the right hemisphere, without using words from the left hemisphere of the brain to describe them.

PAINFUL RELATIONSHIPS
DISMISSIVE AND DISTRACTED ATTACHMENT

   d. In Level 4 stories, participants act-out the story and emotions they are describing using only facial expression, body language, movement or non-verbal interactions with others.

3. To begin the exercise:
   a. Your facilitator will begin the exercise by asking the group if they have ever known anyone who has a dismissive attachment style.
   b. Your facilitator will share one-word descriptions of what dismissive attachment is like – or what it feels like relating to a person with dismissive attachment.
   c. Volunteers may share one-word descriptions of what dismissive attachment is like – or what it feels like trying to relate to a person with dismissive attachment.

4. Your facilitator will tell a Level 4 Dismissive Attachment Story for the entire group that describes what dismissive attachment looks like.

5. Volunteers have the opportunity to tell a Level 4 Dismissive Attachment Story that answers the question, "What does dismissive attachment look like?" Remember to tell these stories using only facial expression, body language, movement or nonverbal interactions. Have fun with this! You are, "Going to Hollywood."

6. Your facilitator will keep track of time for you, and will let you know when it is time to restart the video.

Distracted attachment

Distracted
- Parent sends mixed signals about attachment.
- Interactions tend to be intrusive and are based on parent – not infant state of mind.
- Infant needs sometimes met, sometimes unmet – never knows which.
- Child becomes preoccupied with attachment.

The attachment light: Always On
- It is stuck in a sympathetic dominant state of response to people and relationships.
- High emotions, without ability to quiet self.
- Fear and anger are high arousal states without ability to regulate.
- Impulsive and excitable, little capacity for stress.
- It is hard to live life when always distracted by the possibility of attaching to someone – or something!

PAINFUL RELATIONSHIPS
DISMISSIVE AND DISTRACTED ATTACHMENT

Adult relationships:
- Highly needy, dependent and anxious - focused on receiving comfort for distress.
- Can quickly "attach" in high energy relationships – and appear quite functional – and then overwhelm others.
- Frequent highly emotional displays.
- Can use "neediness" or distress to manipulate others for attention.
- One crisis after another.

What does distracted attachment look like?
- Pause for a Level 4 Distracted Attachment Story.

EXERCISE: TELLING A LEVEL 4 DISTRACTED ATTACHMENT STORY
10 Minutes.

1. For this exercise, it is not necessary to break into small groups.

2. Your facilitator will remind you that Level 4 stories are non-verbal, and are told using facial expressions, body language and movement.

3. To begin the exercise:
   a. Your facilitator will begin the exercise by asking the group if they have ever known anyone who has a distracted attachment style.
   b. Your facilitator will share a one-word description of what distracted attachment is like – or what it feels like trying to relate to a person with distracted attachment.
   c. Volunteers may share one-word descriptions of what distracted attachment is like – or what it feels like trying to relate to a person with distracted attachment.

4. Your facilitator will tell a Level 4 Distracted Attachment Story for the entire group that describes what distracted attachment looks like.

5. Volunteers have the opportunity to tell Level 4 Distracted Attachment Story that answers the question, "What does distracted attachment look like?" Remember to tell these stories using only facial expression, body language, movement or nonverbal interactions with others. Have fun with this! You are, "Going to Hollywood."

6. Your facilitator will keep track of time for you, and will let you know when it is time to restart the video.

PAINFUL RELATIONSHIPS
DISMISSIVE AND DISTRACTED ATTACHMENT

Non-secure attachment is painful.
- Our level of pain is higher than our level of joy.
- This is experienced as trauma and ongoing relational distress.
- But it gets worse!

Non-secure attachment will continue to traumatize and reduce capacity.
- Non-secure attachments lead to a level of pain that exceeds our joy capacity, and this means that we tend to live in ongoing trauma and distress.
- Non-secure attachments continue to make the problem worse because they cause increasing levels of pain and distress – and decrease our levels of joy.
- Our level of trauma worsens.
- We are continually re-traumatized by our non-secure attachments.

Medicate to regulate

BEEPS
- BEEPS are attachments to Behaviors, Events, Experiences, People or Substances that are used to regulate emotions, increase pleasure or decrease pain.

BEEPS
- Attachments to BEEPS help us medicate – to artificially regulate – positive and negative emotions as well as pain.

BEEPS
- Attachments to BEEPS take the place of secure attachments to God and significant others.

BEEPS
- There are many different types of BEEPS. Examples can include:
- Behaviors: Work
- Events: Thrill Seeking
- Experiences: Sex
- People: Relationships
- Substances: Alcohol

Step 4: made a fearless and searching moral inventory of ourselves.

Taking a fearless and searching look at myself.
- Step 4 can only happen when we have attached ourselves to a Power greater than ourselves – someone who is empowered by joy and is genuinely glad to be with us!
- Step 4 is not just about BEEPS.
- Step 4 is about:
  - Identifying the issues and pain that led to BEEPS.
  - Recognizing what my attachments to BEEPS did to my life and relationships.
- Unless I identify the problem and take steps to correct it, I will repeat it!

PAINFUL RELATIONSHIPS
DISMISSIVE AND DISTRACTED ATTACHMENT

Step 5: Admitted to God, to ourselves and to another human being the exact nature of our wrongs.

Getting honest with God, myself and others who are empowered by joy and are willing to share my distress:
- Breaks Isolation.
- Helps break attachments to BEEPS by helping me attach to others.
- Helps build secure, joyful bonds!

Attachment style can become more secure and joyful!

EXERCISE: LEVEL 4+ RETURNING TO JOY FROM NEGATIVE EMOTIONS STORY *30 Minutes*

1. This exercise will help you learn to tell a Level 4+ Return to Joy from Negative Emotions Story.
   a. Your story should describe a time when you experienced the emotion of anger, fear or sadness – and were able to return to joy afterwards.
   b. If you can't remember a time when you experienced these negative emotions and were able to return to joy, explain what you now think you might have been able to do to help you return to joy in the situation you've described. You can also explain how you would like to act in a similar situation that might help you return to joy.
   c. Remember, to the brain, joy means relationship. It means, "Someone is glad to be with me!" As we learn to "Return to Joy," we are discovering how to act like the person God has created us to be – and stay relational with others – when we experience a negative emotion. Returning to joy is about learning to act like ourselves so that we stay connected to others when we are distressed.

2. Locate your "Preparing My Level 4+ Return to Joy Story Worksheet" in your workbook. Your facilitator will take 5 minutes to review the worksheet and characteristics of a Level 4+ Return to Joy from Negative Emotions Story with you. Because this is a story that describes an experience in which you experienced a negative emotion, pay particular attention to the following:
   a. Make sure your story is of moderate intensity so others are not overwhelmed.
   b. Make sure this is a story that you don't need to be guarded in telling.

3. To describe the experience, emotions, body sensations and what you did when you were upset:
   a. Describe the situation. What was occurring when you felt anger, fear or sadness?

PAINFUL RELATIONSHIPS
DISMISSIVE AND DISTRACTED ATTACHMENT

b. List feeling words to describe what anger, fear or sadness felt like to you.

c. Describe the sensations you felt in your body when you were upset. What was going on in your body?

d. What did you do in the story that demonstrates how you like to act when you feel anger, fear or sadness? What did you do in your story that illustrates how you "acted like you" when you were upset?

e. What did you do to return to joy?

f. If you were unable to return to joy in the situation you described, how do you now think you might have been able to "act like yourself" and return to joy? How would you like to act in a similar situation and return to joy? This is helping you answer the question, "What is it like me to do when I am this upset?" How can "acting like you" help you return to joy in the future?

4. Your facilitator will share a 3-minute Level 4+ Return to Joy story with you.

5. You will have 2 minutes to give your facilitator feedback on his/her story.

a. Your facilitator will read each element listed on the worksheet, and ask volunteers to help determine if the story contained each element.

b. Feedback is designed to help a storyteller determine if the story contained each element listed on the worksheet. It should not include criticism or advice about the experience or emotions described in the story.

6. Break into groups of 3 people.

7. Take 5 minutes to complete the "Preparing My Level 4+ Return to Joy Story Worksheet." You may describe a situation in which you experienced an emotion of anger, fear or sadness. Your facilitator will keep track of time for you.

8. Your facilitator will ask for volunteers in each small group to begin telling a Level 4+ Return to Joy Story. You will have 3 minutes to tell your story. Your facilitator will keep track of time for you. If at any point your group is stuck or has a question, please raise your hand, and your facilitator will come help you.

9. After the first joy story, each group can take 2 minutes to give feedback on the story. Use the "Preparing My Level 4+ Return to Joy Story Worksheet" as a guideline to help the storyteller discover if they were able to share all the elements of a 4+ story that are listed on the worksheet. Be encouraging and positive! Your facilitator will keep track of time for you, and let you know when it is time for the next person to share their story.

PAINFUL RELATIONSHIPS
DISMISSIVE AND DISTRACTED ATTACHMENT

10. Your facilitator will let you know when it is time for a second person in each small group to begin their 3-minute Level 4+ Return to Joy Story, followed by 2 minutes of feedback. Your facilitator will keep track of time for you and let you know when it is time for the next person to share their story.

11. Your facilitator will let you know when it is time for the third person in each small group to begin their 3-minute Level 4+ Return to Joy Story, followed by 2 minutes of feedback. Your facilitator will keep track of time for you.

12. At the conclusion of the exercise, participants may remain in their small groups. If time permits, your facilitator will ask volunteers to share about their experience with the entire group. Use one word to describe how it felt to share these stories.

CLOSE THE GROUP WITH PRAYER

PREPARING MY 4+ RETURN TO JOY STORY WORKSHEET

1. This story has a moderate feeling level and is not too intense ☐

2. I have told this story before ☐

3. I do not need to be guarded in telling this story ☐

4. This story is autobiographical (I am involved in the story) ☐

5. This story illustrates a specific feeling ☐

6. I will show the authentic emotion on my face and in my voice ☐

7. I will maintain eye contact while storytelling ☐

8. Briefly describe the situation:

9. Feeling words for this story:

10. During this story my body felt:

11. The things I did in this story that demonstrate how I like to act in this emotion are (or if I did not act like myself at the time, it would have been like me to do this...)

PAINFUL RELATIONSHIPS
DISMISSIVE AND DISTRACTED ATTACHMENT

OPTIONAL EXERCISES

EXERCISE: RUNNING TO STAND STILL *25 Minutes*

1. Break into small groups of 3-5 people.

2. In this exercise, you will be using the song "Running to Stand Still," which is about a person who is using heroin. The goal of this exercise is to help you apply the information you've learned about non-secure attachments to both BEEPS, and to the relational trauma that results from attachments to BEEPS.

3. Your facilitator may share this song with you in audio or video format – or may read the song lyrics to you.

4. As you listen to the song, pay attention to:

   a. The relationship the woman in the song has with heroin.

   b. The relationship the woman in the story has to the person who is telling the story.

5. When the song is finished, you will have 15 minutes to share the answers to these questions with your group:

   a. How did the woman's attachment to heroin affect her?

   b. How do you think the woman's use of heroin affected her relationship with the person telling the story? Was her attachment with this person secure or non-secure? Why?

   c. Your facilitator will help you by keeping track of time.

6. After 15 minutes of sharing, you may remain in your groups, and your facilitator will lead you in a short relaxation exercise.

EXERCISE: LEARNING TO BREATHE DEEPLY *2 Minutes*

1. Follow your facilitator's instructions as you do this exercise.

2. Remain in your small groups. Stand up, and make sure that you have 3-4 feet of clear space around you.

3. Imagine that you are a marionette – a puppet – with a string running from the base of your spine to the top of your head. Imagine that the string is gently pulled upwards and your back, neck and head are perfectly aligned. Your head is at rest and comfortably settled in line with your back and spine. You are looking forward, and your head is settled in comfortably.

4. Bend your knees slightly. You are standing still in a comfortable position.

5. Place your hand over your stomach.

6. Take such a deep breath that you feel your stomach expand as you breathe. Follow your facilitator's instructions as you breathe deeply for a few moments.

7. Your facilitator will keep track of time for you as you relax and breathe deeply.

PAINFUL RELATIONSHIPS
DISMISSIVE AND DISTRACTED ATTACHMENT

QUESTIONS FOR FURTHER DISCUSSION OR FOLLOW-UP

1. How do non-secure attachments form?

2. How would you describe the attachment Adam, Eve and God shared before the fall?

3. What happened to Adam and Eve's attachment with God after the fall?

4. As a result of the fall, Adam and Eve began to relate to God and each other through:
   a. Fear
   b. Shame
   c. Covering Up
   d. Hiding and Denial
   e. Blaming and Accusing
   f. Anger
   g. Sadness

   How have these negative emotions and behaviors each affected your relationship with God – and other relationships that are important to you? Be very specific.

5. Please list 5 characteristics of a dismissive attachment.

6. Do you know someone (including yourself) who has a dismissive attachment? How does this attachment style make it difficult to develop secure attachments? Be specific.

7. From what you learned in this week's lesson, how does a person with a dismissive attachment typically deal with conflict?

8. Why might a person with a dismissive attachment tend to develop a BEEPS with work?

9. Please list 5 characteristics of a distracted attachment.

10. Do you know someone (including yourself) who has a distracted attachment? How does this attachment style make it difficult to develop secure attachments? Be specific.

11. From what you learned in this week's lesson, how does a person with a distracted attachment typically deal with conflict?

12. Why might a person with a distracted attachment tend to develop a BEEPS with relationships?

13. Why do non-secure attachments lead to more trauma and distress in relationships?

14. Why is it important to identify issues of pain, attachment and BEEPS in our lives?

15. How does "getting honest" about our pain, attachments and BEEPS with someone else who is empowered by joy help us in our recovery?

16. What did you learn from the "Running to Stand Still" Exercise?

PAINFUL RELATIONSHIPS
DISMISSIVE AND DISTRACTED ATTACHMENT

1. How did you feel during the "Running to Stand Still" exercise? Has your use of BEEPS caused your life to stand still – or have your attachments to BEEPS taken you backwards? Who did you identify with more in the song: The heroin user – or the person in relationship with them?

2. Which of these emotions and behaviors discussed in this week's lesson have been difficult for you?
   - Fear
   - Shame
   - Covering Up
   - Hiding and Denial
   - Blaming and Accusing
   - Anger
   - Sadness

3. How have these affected your life and relationships with God and other people? Be specific.

4. Have you ever used BEEPS to deal with these negative emotions and behaviors? Which BEEPS have you used to help you with these feelings and behaviors?

5. Do you think that your own non-secure attachments have caused you pain? What kind of pain did you experience? How long have you had this pain?

6. Do you have a dismissive or distracted attachment style? How has this affected your life, relationships and attachments to BEEPS?

7. Did your mom, dad or the person who took care of you when you were growing up have dismissive or distracted attachments?

8. What do you expect from other people? How do you expect them to act and behave towards you? When did you learn to expect these things from others?

9. How long have you lived in the pain of non-secure attachment? Can you remember a time when you did not feel the pain of non-secure attachments?

10. Have you ever violated your own values through your use of BEEPS? Be specific. How did it happen – and did you feel guilty about it later? Do you continue to violate your own values with BEEPS today? How do you resolve – or medicate – your feelings of guilt about this?

11. When we are attached to BEEPS, we lose things that are important to us. How has your use of BEEPS caused you loss in these areas? Be specific.
    a. Relationships
    b. Work
    c. Opportunities
    d. Health
    e. Finances
    f. Possessions

PAINFUL RELATIONSHIPS
DISMISSIVE AND DISTRACTED ATTACHMENT

12. When we are growing in our attachments with BEEPS, we tend to deny that we have a problem with BEEPS. We also tend to blame the problems BEEPS causes – that are too big to deny - on other people, places and things. Make a list of all the excuses that you've used to justify your use of BEEPS. Make a second list of all of the people, places and things that you've blamed for the problems BEEPS have caused.

13. When we've blamed other people, places and things for our problems, it is easy to develop resentments towards them. Make a list of the people that you've resented – for the problems BEEPS have caused you.

14. What is the worst moment of your attachment with BEEPS that you can remember? Describe it in detail.

15. How can admitting to God, yourself and another human being the pain and problems you've inventoried in these questions help your recovery?

16. Why is it important that the person you share these problems with be empowered by joy – and willing to share your distress? How can that help you?

17. Do you know anybody who is empowered by joy, and would be willing to share your distress? Who are they?

    What do you think would happen if you shared the pain and problems you've identified with them?

7 TOXIC RELATIONSHIPS
DISORGANIZED ATTACHMENT AND TRAUMA

OPEN THE GROUP WITH PRAYER

EXERCISE: APPRECIATION EXERCISE *10 Minutes*

1. Break into small groups of 3-5 people.

2. Your facilitator will ask each person to think about either:
   a. An experience they had with a person they especially appreciated in the past week.
   b. An experience they had with God this week that was especially meaningful.

3. Your facilitator will ask you each to take one minute to share with your group about the experience you had this week. Remember to:
   a. Maintain eye contact while sharing.
   b. Identify the person and experience that you appreciated
   c. Describe what emotions you felt during your experience.
   d. Describe what your body felt during that experience.

4. Your facilitator will help you by keeping track of time.

5. When each group is finished, your facilitator may ask volunteers to share how they feel after the exercise with the entire group. Use one or two words to describe your feelings.

TODAY´S LESSON: Disorganized Attachment and Trauma

CLASS NOTES: Disorganized Attachment and Trauma

A quick review

There are four attachment styles:
- Secure
- Dismissive
- Distracted
- Disorganized

TOXIC RELATIONSHIPS
DISORGANIZED ATTACHMENT AND TRAUMA

Secure attachment:
- Secure attachment results from high joy capacity and synchronized bonds.
- How do non-secure attachments form?

Non-secure attachments result from:
- Lack of joy capacity.
- Lack of synchronization.
- Getting stuck in pain without the ability to return to joy.
- These keep us further disconnected from joyful relationships with God and others.

After the Fall
- Then the eyes of both of them were opened, and they knew that they were naked; and they sewed fig leaves together and made themselves coverings And they heard the sound of the Lord God walking in the garden in the cool of the day, and Adam and his wife hid themselves from the presence of the Lord God among the trees of the garden. Then the Lord God called to Adam and said to him, "Where are you?" So he said, "I heard Your voice in the garden, and I was afraid because I was naked; and I hid myself." And He said, "Who told you that you were naked? Have you eaten from the tree of which I commanded you that you should not eat?" Then the man said, "The woman whom You gave to be with me, she gave me of the tree, and I ate." And the Lord God said to the woman, "What is this you have done?" The woman said, "The serpent deceived me, and I ate." Genesis 3:7-10. NKJV.

The relational consequences of the Fall include:
- Dismissive attachment.
- Distracted attachment.
- Disorganized attachment.

Disorganized attachment
- Relationship with parent/caregiver is the source of attachment and terror.
- Fear/terror of the attachment figure offers no comfort or synchronization – no soothing.
- Parent exhibits chaotic or disorganized behavior.
- Infant can't make sense of the "come here – go away" relationship.

Parent state
- Parents themselves have disorganized attachment, fear-based, dissociative, or disoriented behaviors.
- May include addictive behaviors.
- Physical, sexual, emotional abuse.
- 80% of abused children have disorganized attachment.

TOXIC RELATIONSHIPS
DISORGANIZED ATTACHMENT AND TRAUMA

Adult relationships
- Highest likelihood of clinical problems.
- Hostile and aggressive with peers, controlling, difficult social relationships.
- Unregulated emotion followed by withdrawal.
- Abusive patterns of behavior.
- Virtual Other seen as important but terrifying, causing future relationships to fail, and increasing internal disorganization.
- Level 2 pain: pervasive fear and fear bonded relationships.

Domestic violence and disorganized attachment
- When the abuser feels needed – or asked to attach in any way – he or she is triggered into fear.
- The need could be anything from grocery money to affection.
- That fear may explode into rage – to make the pain stop and protect himself or herself.
- This pattern is highly likely if the abuser's spouse has distracted or disorganized attachment.
- You can't stop the violence by being a better wife, trying harder, not making him mad or "biblical submission."

Attachment and God
- Dismissive:
  - Avoidant and withdrawn
  - God at a distance, flat affect
- Distracted:
  - Anxious, needy
  - Performance and approval, high arousal, manipulative
- Disorganized:
  - Terror and fear
  - God is terrifying
  - Cults, spiritual abuse

The impacts of trauma and weak attachment on relationships
- Patterns of insecure or disorganized relationships continue throughout life, damaging relationships with friends, spouses and children.
- Series of ongoing unsatisfying relationships.
- Repeated relationship failures.
- Lack of joy-filled, mutually satisfying intimacy.
- Tend to over-react or withdraw from relationships.
- Overly dependent and needy or isolated and distant.
- Relationships are a source of pain – not comfort.
- Lack of mutual mind and synchronization.
- BEEPS

What does disorganized attachment look like?
- Pause for a Level 4 Disorganized Attachment Story.

TOXIC RELATIONSHIPS
DISORGANIZED ATTACHMENT AND TRAUMA

YOUR NOTES

EXERCISE: TELLING A LEVEL 4 DISORGANIZED ATTACHMENT STORY
10 Minutes

1. For this exercise, it is not necessary to break into small groups.

2. Your facilitator will explain Level 4 stories.
   a. Level 4 stories are non-verbal stories that are told without using words.
   b. Level 4+ stories combine elements of both the left hemisphere (words) and right hemisphere (emotions) of the brain.
   c. Level 4 stories express the experiences, feelings, and sensations of the right hemisphere, without using words from the left hemisphere of the brain to describe them.
   d. In Level 4 stories, participants act out the story and emotions they are describing using only facial expression, body language, movement or non-verbal interactions with others.

3. To begin the exercise:
   a. Your facilitator will begin the exercise by asking the group if they have ever known anyone who has a disorganized attachment style.
   b. Your facilitator will share a one-word description of what disorganized attachment is like – or what it feels like trying to relate to a person with disorganized attachment.
   c. Volunteers share one-word descriptions of what disorganized attachment is like – or what it feels like trying to relate to a person with disorganized attachment.

4. Your facilitator will tell a Level 4 Disorganized Attachment Story for the entire group that describes what disorganized attachment looks like.

5. Volunteers have the opportunity to tell Level 4 Disorganized Attachment Story that answers the question, "What does disorganized attachment look like?" Remember to tell these stories using only facial expression, body language, movement or non-verbal interactions. Have fun with this! You are, "Going to Hollywood."

6. Your facilitator will keep track of time for you, and will let you know when it is time to restart the video.

Dismissive, distracted and disorganized attachments are painful.
   • Our level of pain is higher than our level of joy.
   • This is experienced as trauma and ongoing relational distress.
   • But it gets worse!

TOXIC RELATIONSHIPS
DISORGANIZED ATTACHMENT AND TRAUMA

Non-secure attachments produce ongoing trauma.
- Non-secure attachments lead to a level of pain that exceeds our joy capacity, and this means that we tend to live in ongoing trauma and distress.
- Non-secure attachments continue to make the problem worse because they cause increasing levels of pain and distress – and decrease our levels of joy.
- Our level of trauma worsens.
- We are continually re-traumatized by our non-secure attachments.

Lack of secure attachment diminishes capacity for life and relationships.
- Non-secure attachment hurts relationships throughout my lifespan.

Diminished capacity: trauma

What is trauma?
- Trauma is an experience or series of experiences that overwhelm our emotional capacity to handle the experience. As a result of being overwhelmed, we are diminished as persons, are not able to "act like ourselves" and are unable to live from the heart that Jesus gave us.

The issues with trauma:
- How far did you fall?
- What did you hit?
- How was your landing?

Trauma and suffering
- Trauma is anything that reduces who we are, or who we understand ourselves to be. The unregulated emotional intensity of the traumatic event reduces us to less than we were before.
- Suffering: "Those who suffer are at peace with themselves and the world. Sufferers may find their capacities drastically reduced, even to the point of death, but the continue to be themselves with the capacity and dominion they have left." Thomas Gerlach
- Jesus is our example.

Type A trauma
- The absence of necessary good things.

Type A: the absence of necessary good things:
- Inhibits the development of capacity.
- Abandonment, rejection, malnutrition.
- Isolation, lack of love.
- No encouragement.
- Insecure attachments.

Type B trauma
- Bad things that happen.

TOXIC RELATIONSHIPS
DISORGANIZED ATTACHMENT AND TRAUMA

Type B: bad things that happen
- Overwhelms existing capacity
- Murder, rape, assault
- Molestation, incest, child abuse
- Humiliation, betrayal, contempt
- "First-person shooter" video games

The loss of the ability to regulate the intensity of feelings is the most far-reaching effect of early trauma and neglect. (van der Kolk)

Medicate to regulate

BEEPS
- BEEPS are attachments to Behaviors, Events, Experiences, People or Substances that are used to regulate emotions, increase pleasure or decrease pain.

BEEPS
- Attachments to BEEPS help us medicate – to artificially regulate – positive and negative emotions as well as pain.

BEEPS
- Attachments to BEEPS take the place of secure attachments to God and significant others.

BEEPS
- There are many different types of BEEPS. Examples can include:
- Behaviors: Work
- Events: Thrill Seeking
- Experiences: Sex
- People: Relationships
- Substances: Alcohol

The BEEPS cycle is relational
- Attachment pain > reduced capacity > BEEPS attachments > damaged relationships > attachment pain.
- That's why recovery must also be relational.

The Twelve Steps are a relational program of recovery.
- Relationship with God
  - Steps 1, 2, 3 and 11.
- Relationship with Self
  - Steps 4, 5, 6, 7 and 10.
- Relationship with Others
  - Steps 8, 9, and 12.
- When these relationships grow in balance, our recovery will also remain balanced.
- Without growth in all 3 of these relationships, recovery will be out of balance, and will not stand.

TOXIC RELATIONSHIPS
DISORGANIZED ATTACHMENT AND TRAUMA

When we apply the Twelve Steps relationally to attachment pain
- Our hearts can heal from trauma.

We can attach to others in joy
- Our recovery is Thriving!

EXERCISE: INTRODUCTION TO THE IMMANUEL PROCESS *30 Minutes*

1. Break into small groups of 3-5 people.

2. Your facilitator will introduce you to the Immanuel Process Exercise. This exercise will help you recognize times in your life in which you felt particularly close with Jesus – or were aware of His presence.

   a. "Immanuel" means "God with us."

   b. Jesus has promised to always be with us – Matt 28:20.

   c. It is possible for Jesus to be with us – and be totally unaware of His presence. It is also possible for Jesus to help us recognize His presence. (Luke 24:13-32).

   d. Recalling our experience of God is scriptural. (John 14:26, Matt 16:9, Psalm 42).

   e. Just as trauma can be a part of our memory – so can the presence of Jesus.

3. Your facilitator will share with you a time when he/she experienced God's presence in a way that was powerful, meaningful and memorable. He/she will maintain eye contact with you as he/she describes:

   a. What happened in the experience he/she is remembering.

   b. What emotions he/she felt.

   c. What his/her body felt like when he/she was with Jesus.

   d. What he/she did when he/she experienced His presence.

   e. How does it feels to be with Jesus.

4. Your facilitator will ask each of you to close your eyes, and ask Jesus to help you remember a time when you felt very close to Him. As your eyes are closed, your facilitator may help you by quietly asking the questions listed below. You do not need to answer these questions aloud; the questions are only to help you focus on the memory of your experience with Jesus. Your facilitator will help you by keeping track of time during this portion of the exercise, and let you know when it is time to open your eyes.

   a. What is happening in the experience you are remembering?

   b. What emotions are you feeling?

   c. What does your body feel like when you are with Jesus?

   d. What are you doing in that memory?

   e. How does it feel to be with Jesus?

TOXIC RELATIONSHIPS
DISORGANIZED ATTACHMENT AND TRAUMA

5. Your facilitator will let you know when to open your eyes, and ask for volunteers to begin sharing for 2 minutes about their experience with their small group. Your facilitator will help you keep track of time as you share. Remember to stay relational by making eye contact as you describe:

  a. The experience with Jesus you just remembered.

  b. The emotions you felt in the memory.

  c. What your body felt like.

  d. What you did when you felt the presence of Jesus.

  e. How does it feel to remember this experience with Jesus?

6. When each participant has had the opportunity to share their experience with their small group, your facilitator will ask volunteers to describe what it feels like to experience the presence of Jesus with the entire group. Use one or two words to describe your feelings.

CLOSE THE GROUP WITH PRAYER

TOXIC RELATIONSHIPS
DISORGANIZED ATTACHMENT AND TRAUMA

QUESTIONS FOR FURTHER DISCUSSION OR FOLLOW-UP

1. How do you define disorganized attachment?

2. What characterizes a relationship between parent and their child in a disorganized attachment?

3. What issues in the life of a parent can lead to the development of a disorganized attachment?

4. Why do you think that addictions can play a role in the development of a disorganized attachment?
   Can addictions lead to a disorganized attachment?

5. Why do disorganized attachments lead to such toxic relationships?

6. Have you ever been in a relationship with a person who had a disorganized attachment? What was that relationship like?

7. Why does "biblical submission" fail as a strategy for dealing with domestic violence?

8. Have you been able to identify your own attachment style? How has this influenced your ability to develop a secure attachment with God?

9. Has your own non-secure attachment style interfered with your ability to have satisfying relationships in life? How have these non-secure attachments affected your attachments with others throughout your life? Be as specific as you can.

10. How do you define trauma? Why is an understanding of capacity so essential for this definition?

11. What is the difference between trauma and suffering? How could Jesus have endured the cross – but still continue to act like himself in the midst of His suffering?

12. What is the difference between Trauma A and Trauma B? Why is it important to understand the difference?

13. How do Trauma A and Trauma B each affect our capacity?

14. Have you experienced Trauma A or Trauma B? How have these influenced your capacity, life and relationships?

15. Why is it so important for recovery to be relational?

16. How can the Twelve Steps help keep our recovery balanced?

17. What did you experience during The Immanuel Process exercise? How did you feel during the exercise?

TOXIC RELATIONSHIPS
DISORGANIZED ATTACHMENT AND TRAUMA

OPTIONAL 12-STEP QUESTIONS

1. Why is the BEEPS cycle relational?

2. Did one or both of your parents use BEEPS? How did this influence your attachments with them? Were their attachments with you disorganized?

3. Have you ever had a truly secure and satisfying relationship – or have your relationships been continually sabotaged by non-secure attachments? Explain.

4. How did you handle the relational pain when relationships did not work – or were unsatisfying? What BEEPS did you use to medicate the pain?

5. Has your use of BEEPS made your attachment pain worse? How?

6. How has your use of BEEPS diminished your capacity for life and relationships?

7. Would you describe your attachment with BEEPS as dismissive, distracted or disorganized? Why?

8. Has your use of BEEPS caused your relationships with others to become increasingly dismissive, distracted or disorganized? Why – or why not?

9. How do you define trauma? How has your use of BEEPS been traumatic to you and others?

10. Have you experienced Trauma A and/or B? List at least 3 ways in which these have affected your life, capacity and relationships.

11. Do you use BEEPS to medicate the pain of Trauma A or Trauma B? How has this diminished your capacity and made your level of pain worse?

12. Why is it so important for your relationships with God, yourself and others to grow in recovery? What happens if these relationships get out of balance?

13. How can the Twelve Steps help your relationships to remain balanced as your recovery grows?

14. What did you experience during the Immanuel Process exercise? How did you feel during the exercise? How were these emotions different from the feelings you get after using BEEPS?

TOXIC RELATIONSHIPS
DISORGANIZED ATTACHMENT AND TRAUMA

SOLUTIONS COME FIRST

Our body has probably been damaged by the effects of our attachments to substances like alcohol or other drugs, food, or sex. Some of us have carried the extreme weight of unhealthy attachments to people with addictions. While they numbed themselves – we've been awake and feeling every ounce of betrayal, hurt, rage, sadness and disappointment possible. The physical and psychological effects of this – and other types of trauma and abuse have crippled our ability to think clearly, destroyed our ability to trust and have life-giving relationships with others, and have probably ravaged our bodies with a variety of disorders related to stress and anxiety. To make it worse, we've probably heard others tell us that "things will get better," but right now, in these early days, this just seems impossible! We want to feel better – and the sooner the better!

Our problems may not have seemed quite so bad before…but now that we are aware of the battering, bruising and incredible physical, mental and emotional pain we've lived in, we are crying out for relief and answers. When our pain finally gets our attention, we are often not sure where to go or what to do…but we know that we are tired of being tied to our addictions and pain while they shred our body, our dignity and violate every good thing in our life.

For many of us, our coping strategies worked for awhile but gradually led to a powerful downward spiral that baffled, confused and terrified us. Perhaps the most terrifying of all was the realization that we were no longer in control of our lives – and that addiction, abuse or traumas were actually driving the horses that dragged us behind them. Only when the pain of denying or ignoring the problems became greater than our fear of admitting and feeling our pain – did we become open to ask for help.

In our distress, most of us start trying to figure out who to blame for the way our lives have turned out. The most frequent targets of our wrath are usually ourselves and those who have been close to us. Questions, recriminations, and guilt overwhelm us like a flood. Looking back at our attachments to alcohol, drugs or other addictive behaviors, we rage against ourselves wondering things like, "How could I have been so stupid! Why did I keep on using? Why couldn't I just stop? Why did I stay in this relationship?" Some of us who have been unimaginably violated by traumas and abuses cry out, "How did this happen? How could they do this? Why didn't I stop them? Why didn't they protect me?"

Those of us who have walked the journey of recovery for many years know that these questions are important and need to be answered. But we've also learned that the temporary satisfaction we gain from figuring out whom to blame does not help us heal from the pain of addiction, traumas and abuse. Even if we are right – and correctly figure out whose fault our predicament is – blame only gives our outrage more energy, but does nothing to help heal our mind, body and heart. You will find that the more effort, energy and time you spend trying to analyze your problems, the more discouraged, depressed and anxious about your future you will become. Answers to your questions will come with time – but they will emerge as you focus on learning and applying solutions to your problems – and not because you become an expert at problem analysis!

Wise Thoughts About Group Rules

1. You can help build joy and a recovery community for you and others. Your community thrives when you keep the personal information Restarting members share in your group confidential. Do not share it with others. Your facilitator will help you and others stay safe by reporting child or elder abuse – and any imminent danger to you or to the person or property of others.

2. Take every opportunity to build joy – and practice your joy-building skills in Restarting.

3. Express appreciation to each other frequently.

4. When you are glad to be with others, it helps them feel like they belong – and helps build a Restarting community that is joyful.

5. Supportive listening helps others share, heal and feel comfortable. It's a lot harder for others to build joy with you when you are offering criticism or advice. The directions that accompany each exercise will help you learn to offer constructive and helpful feedback that builds joy.

6. Sharing is strongly encouraged, but not required.

7. By following your facilitator's instructions and the directions in your workbook, you will help keep your group on track, learn new Restarting skills, and help provide enough time for everyone to share.

8. Encourage others to return to Restarting.

9. Following your facilitator's directions to complete all Restarting exercises in groups of 3-5 people will help you build the kind of joy that is powerful – and safe – for you and everyone else.

10. It is very difficult for you and for others to create belonging if you arrive for group intoxicated, so if you come to group "under the influence", you won't be able to participate in Restarting that evening.

11. Threats, violence and intimidation are a sign that you are overwhelmed – and are actively and intensely overwhelming others. Because these behaviors make Restarting unsafe for others, you will be unable to return to Restarting if you do them.

8 TRAUMA, HOPE AND RECOVERY
TRAUMA

OPEN THE GROUP WITH PRAYER

EXERCISE: A MOMENT WITH JESUS *10 Minutes*

1. Break into small groups of 3-5 people.

2. Your facilitator will ask volunteers to share about a time in the past week when they felt that Jesus was with them. Your facilitator will begin the exercise by sharing a moment from the past week in which he/she was able to perceive the presence of Jesus. Your facilitator will stay relational with you by maintaining eye contact as he/she shares and describes:

   a. The experience he/she had with Jesus.

   b. The emotions he/she felt.

   c. How his/her body felt.

   d. How he/she felt after the experience.

3. Each volunteer can take 2 minutes to share about his/her experience with their small group. Be sure to stay relational by making eye contact as you share your experience with Jesus and describe:

   a. The experience you had with Jesus.

   b. The emotions you felt.

   c. How your body felt.

   d. How you felt after the experience.

4. Your facilitator will help you by keeping track of time.

5. When each group is finished, your facilitator may ask volunteers to share how they feel after the exercise with the entire group. Use one or two words to describe your feelings.

TODAY´S LESSON: Trauma and Recovery

CLASS NOTES: Trauma and Recovery

Attachment: a quick review:
- Secure
- Dismissive
- Distracted
- Disorganized

TRAUMA, HOPE AND RECOVERY
TRAUMA

Secure attachment:
- Secure attachment results from high joy capacity and synchronized bonds.
- How do non-secure attachments form?

After the Fall:
- Then the eyes of both of them were opened, and they knew that they were naked; and they sewed fig leaves together and made themselves coverings. And they heard the sound of the Lord God walking in the garden in the cool of the day, and Adam and his wife hid themselves from the presence of the Lord God among the trees of the garden.
- Then the Lord God called to Adam and said to him, "Where are you?"
- So he said, "I heard Your voice in the garden, and I was afraid because I was naked; and I hid myself."
- And He said, "Who told you that you were naked? Have you eaten from the tree of which I commanded you that you should not eat?"
- Then the man said, "The woman whom You gave to be with me, she gave me of the tree, and I ate."
- And the Lord God said to the woman, "What is this you have done?"
- The woman said, "The serpent deceived me, and I ate." Genesis 3:7-10. NKJV.

Non-secure attachments result from:
- Lack of joy capacity.
- Lack of synchronization.
- Getting stuck in pain without the ability to return to joy.
- These keep us further disconnected from joyful relationships with God and others.

Dismissive attachment: a painful identity
- Avoid relationship
- Low affect
- Negative emotions
- Withdrawal as coping strategy
- Can't synchronize
- Life is safer and feels better alone

Distracted attachment: a painful identity
- Highly needy
- Always trying to attach to receive comfort for distress
- High affect and drama
- Approach as coping strategy
- Frequent crisis
- Can use "neediness" or distress to manipulate others for attention

Disorganized attachment: a painful identity
- Attachment is source of terror and comfort
- High affect/drama and fearful withdrawal or attack
- Very manipulative
- Hostile/aggressive with peers

TRAUMA, HOPE AND RECOVERY
TRAUMA

- Difficult social relationships
- Abuser or abuse victim

Lack of secure attachment diminishes capacity for life and relationships.
- Non-secure attachment hurts relationships throughout my lifespan.

Diminished capacity: ongoing trauma

What is trauma?
- Trauma is an experience or series of experiences that overwhelm our emotional capacity to handle the experience.
- It tends to damage other areas of life related to the initial trauma.
- As a result of being overwhelmed, we are diminished as persons, are not able to "act like ourselves" and are unable to live from the heart that Jesus gave us.

The issues with trauma:
- How far did you fall?
- What did you hit?
- How was your landing?

Trauma and suffering:
- Trauma is anything that reduced who we are, or who we understand ourselves to be. The unregulated emotional intensity of the traumatic event reduces us to less than we were before it.
- Suffering: "Those who suffer are at peace with themselves and the world. Sufferers may find their capacities drastically reduced, even to the point of death, but they continue to be themselves with the capacities and dominion they have left." Thomas Gerlach
- Jesus is our example.

Type A trauma
- The absence of necessary good things.

Type A: the absence of necessary good things
- Inhibits the development of capacity
- Abandonment, rejection, malnutrition
- Isolation, lack of love
- No encouragement
- Insecure attachments

Type B trauma
- Bad things that happen.

Type B: bad things that happen
- Overwhelms existing capacity
- Murder, rape, assault
- Molestation, incest, child abuse
- Humiliation, betrayal, contempt
- "First-person shooter" video games

TRAUMA, HOPE AND RECOVERY
TRAUMA

Trauma A or B can severely impact the control center on multiple levels:
- Level 1: Attachment pain
- Level 2: Pervasive fear
- Level 3: Desynchronized, stuck in negative emotions
- Level 4: Immaturity
- Level 5: Inconsistent identity

Disruption to the control center:
- Degree of pain depends on:
  - Age
  - Severity of trauma
  - Existing capacity
  - Attachments
- It is often sub-cortical.
- May result in unregulated emotions – without the ability to calm yourself.
- Communication between portions of the left and right hemispheres of the brain may temporarily shut down.

Trauma disrupts communication between the left and right hemispheres of the brain.
- Left hemisphere: naming and explaining.
- Right hemisphere: knowing and experience.
- The first indication of being overwhelmed (as well as the persistent evidence of trauma) is a desynchronization or disconnection between the right and left hemispheres of the brain when what we are experiencing does not fit our explanations about ourselves and our life.
- The right side of the brain takes over until the distress has passed.

Loss of control:
- The prefrontal cortex loses control of the amygdala.

Communication breakdown: right hemisphere
- If things get worse, communication with the PFC breaks down when the capacity and the control center are overwhelmed.
- The amygdala (sub-cortical) runs the control center until the distress/trauma is over.

When the amygdala is in charge, we visit one of these desks:
- The Flight Desk:
  - Run and get away.
- The Fight Desk:
  - Protect ourself and make the distress stop.
- The Check Out Desk:
  - Shut down until it's over.
- The Library Desk:
  - Study the problem.

Fear-based thinking dominates.
- The portions of the control center and right brain that are more concerned with primitive impulses of survival often dominate.

TRAUMA, HOPE AND RECOVERY
TRAUMA

- Fear based thinking: Running on adrenaline - terror/rage
  - I can become a non-relational human being
  - I do not think or act like a person
  - I cannot distinguish people from objects
  - I am not open to logic, reason or persuasion – facts don't work!

Dissociation
- If the trauma and terror/rage persist, I shut down into an energy conservation state known as dissociation.
- "An energy conservation withdrawal state in which all possible brain circuits are shut down after a massive desynchronization. Only the amygdala which can't be shut down is ON, along with the associated regions. This is experienced as "death" at the moment there should have been rest." Dr. Alan Schore.
- It is like dying.

In dissociation:
- We have exhausted our sympathetic arousal of terror and rage.
- A parasympathetic shut down occurs to save energy.

Dissociation is sub-cortical
- It is below our conscious control.

Once dissociation is used to replace rest, the brain will tend to dissociate – rather than learn to rest in the future.
- The dissociative child learns to shut down instead of rest.
- Not learning to rest is bad for us – and for our brain!
- Not learning to rest (serotonin regulation) is the main predictor of mental illness during the remainder of life.

When the left hemisphere is not communicating with the right hemisphere, our explicit memory is impaired.
- I may no longer remember or be aware that I am present in the trauma, or that it happened to me.

The loss of the ability to regulate the intensity of feelings is the most far-reaching effect of early trauma and neglect. (van der kolk)

Positive feeling traumas and euphoric recall:
- Not all traumas are the result of negative feelings.
- The intensity of positive feelings – or the memory of those feelings - can be traumatic when they overwhelm our capacity to handle those positive feelings.
- This is a critical issue in BEEPS and relapse.

Medicate to regulate

BEEPS
- There are many different types of BEEPS. Examples can include:
- Behaviors: Work

TRAUMA, HOPE AND RECOVERY
TRAUMA

- Events: Thrill Seeking
- Experiences: Sex
- People: Relationships
- Substances: Alcohol

The BEEPS cycle is relational
- Attachment pain> reduced capacity> BEEPS attachments > damaged relationships >attachment pain.
- This cycle of pain must be addressed in recovery.**The Twelve Steps can help us address the pain and trauma of the BEEPS cycle:**
- Relationship with God
  - Steps 1, 2, 3 and 11.
- Relationship with self
  - Steps 4, 5, 6, 7 and 10.
- Relationship with others
  - Steps 8, 9, and 12.
- When these relationships grow in balance, our recovery will also remain balanced.
- Without growth in all 3 of these relationships, recovery will be out of balance, and will not stand.
- The 12 Steps can help us address the pain and trauma of the BEEPS cycle only if we are part of a joyful community that can help us heal and grow through our pain.

Thriving builds joyful community to help us heal and grow through the pains of trauma and addiction.
- Unlike many Twelve Step and self-help recovery groups, Thriving specifically identifies Trauma A and Trauma B as significant factors relating to both addiction and relapse.
- Thriving teaches participants the joy and relationship building skills that the brain needs to heal – and remain sober – through the development of secure, healthy attachments with God and others in a mature, life-giving community.

EXERCISE: THE IMMANUEL PROCESS *45 Minutes*

IMMANUEL PROCESS PART 1

1. Break into small groups of 3-5 people.

2. Your facilitator will introduce you to the Immanuel Process exercise. This exercise will help you recognize times in your life in which you felt particularly close with Jesus – or were aware of His presence. (2-3 Minutes)

    a. "Immanuel" means "God with us."

    b. Jesus has promised to always be with us – Matt 28:20.

    c. It is possible for Jesus to be with us and be totally unaware of His presence. It is also possible for Jesus to help us recognize His presence. (Luke 24:13-32).

TRAUMA, HOPE AND RECOVERY
TRAUMA

    d. Recalling our experience with God is scriptural. (John 14:26, Matt. 16:9, Ps. 42).

    e. Just as trauma can be a part of our memory – so can the presence of Jesus.

3. Your facilitator will share with you a time when he/she experienced the presence of God in a way that was powerful, meaningful and memorable. He/she will maintain eye contact with you as they describe: (2 Minutes)

    a. What happened in the experience he/she is remembering.

    b. What emotions he/she felt.

    c. What his/her body felt like when he/she was with Jesus.

    d. What he/she did when he/she experienced His presence.

    e. How did it feel to be with Jesus?

4. Your facilitator will ask each of you to close your eyes, and ask Jesus to help you remember a time when you felt very close to Him. As your eyes are closed, your facilitator may help you by quietly asking the questions listed below. You do not need to answer these questions aloud; the questions are only to help you focus on the memory of your experience with Jesus. Your facilitator will help you by keeping track of time during this portion of the exercise, and let you know when it is time to open your eyes. (3 Minutes)

    a. What is happening in the experience you are remembering?

    b. What emotions are you feeling?

    c. What does your body feel like when you are with Jesus?

    d. What are you doing in that memory?

    e. How does it feel to be with Jesus?

5. Your facilitator will let you know when to open your eyes, and ask for volunteers to begin sharing for 2 minutes about their experience with their small group. Your facilitator will help you keep track of time as you share. Remember to stay relational by making eye contact as you describe: (10 Minutes)

    a. The experience with Jesus you just remembered.

    b. The emotions you felt in the memory.

    c. What your body felt like.

    d. What you did when you felt the presence of Jesus.

    e. How does it feel to remember this experience with Jesus?

6. When each participant has had the opportunity to share their experience with their small group, your facilitator will ask volunteers to describe what it feels like to experience the presence of Jesus with the entire group.   Use one or two words to describe your feelings. (1-2 Minutes)

TRAUMA, HOPE AND RECOVERY
TRAUMA

EXERCISE: IMMANUEL PROCESS PART 2

1. Remain in your small groups of 3-5 people.

2. Your facilitator will introduce the second part of this exercise that involves learning to move from a peaceful place with Jesus in which you can perceive His presence into areas of life that do not feel peaceful or in which you haven't been able to perceive that He is with you. DO NOT TRY THIS SECOND PART IF YOU DID NOT EXPERIENCE JESUS PRESENCE IN THE FIRST PART OF THIS EXERCISE. (5-10 Minutes)

3. Your facilitator will also let you know that if at any point you feel stuck or distressed, you can return to the memory of the joyful and peaceful memory of the experience with Jesus that you described in the first part of the exercise.

4. Your facilitator will also explain the reasons that some people may have difficulty experiencing the presence of Jesus in painful areas of life. These include:

   a. Some participants may not be able to describe a "peak experience" or time in which they felt particularly close with Jesus. This may be due to a variety of factors, including the presence of exceptionally severe trauma that has formed blockages that keep them from perceiving His presence. These participants can be encouraged that Jesus often wants to help them by bringing other people into their life that can help them resolve these blockages.

   b. Some may have never asked Jesus to be part of their life, and as a result, have had no real awareness of His presence. It may be appropriate to ask these participants if they would like to invite Jesus to help them perceive His presence.

   c. Some participants may experience strong fear that keeps them from perceiving Jesus' presence in non-peaceful areas of life. Because their fear makes it difficult for them to perceive Jesus in distressing areas of life, these participants are encouraged to meditate upon the peaceful experience they meditated on in the first part of the exercise.

5. Your facilitator will ask each of you to close your eyes, and think again about the time you felt very close to Jesus. Your facilitator will help you by quietly asking the questions listed below. Participants who were able to perceive the presence of Jesus in the first part of this exercise are invited to ask Him these questions. You do not need to answer these questions aloud; these are questions for you to ask Jesus. As you ask these questions, be sensitive to His presence and leading. After each question, wait for Jesus to help you. These questions are: (5 Minutes)

   a. Jesus, is there a non-peaceful place in my life that you want to show me?

TRAUMA, HOPE AND RECOVERY
TRAUMA

    b. Where are you in this place? Will you help me to perceive your presence here?

    c. Jesus, what is keeping me from perceiving your presence here?

    d. Jesus, is there anything you want me to do now?

    e. If you did not find a peaceful memory with Jesus in the first part of this Immanuel Process exercise continue looking for a peaceful place with God rather than asking about the non-peaceful places in your life.

6. During this portion of the exercise, your facilitator may help you by reminding you that you can return to the joyful and peaceful memory of your experience with Jesus that you described in the first part of this exercise.

7. At the conclusion of this exercise, your facilitator will invite you to return to the peaceful and joyful memory that you described in the first part of this exercise.

8. Your facilitator will let you know when to open your eyes, and ask for volunteers to begin sharing for 2 minutes in their small group about their experience. Your facilitator will help you keep track of time as you share. Remember to stay relational by making eye contact as you describe: (10 Minutes)

    a. The experience with Jesus you just remembered.

    b. The emotions you felt in the memory.

    c. What your body felt like.

    d. What you did when you felt the presence of Jesus.

    e. How does it feel to remember this experience with Jesus?

9. When everyone has had the opportunity to share in their small group, your facilitator may ask volunteers to share one or two words with the entire group to describe their experience with Jesus in the second part of the exercise. (2 Minutes).

CLOSE THE GROUP WITH PRAYER

TRAUMA, HOPE AND RECOVERY
TRAUMA

1. Why is a painful identity a problem that is common to dismissive, distracted and disorganized attachments?

2. What happens to the development of capacity with Trauma A? What happens to existing capacity with Trauma B?

3. What do you think happens to our capacity when we experience both Trauma A and Trauma B?

4. What effect does trauma have on each level of the control center?

5. How does trauma influence our ability to self-regulate emotions?

6. Why do you think it is important that many of trauma's impacts on us are sub-cortical?

7. What happens to communication between the left and right hemispheres of the brain when we experience trauma?

8. Being so upset that we "can't think straight" can describe the type of distress we experience when communication breaks down between the left and right hemispheres of the brain. Have you ever had this experience? Describe your experience. What did you do when you were this upset? From what you now know about recovery and the brain, how would you have liked to be able to handle the experience?

9. What can happen to communication between the right pre-frontal cortex and the amygdala if our level of distress is too overwhelming?

10. What are the four things that we can do when we are overwhelmed and the amygdala is in charge?

11. Have you ever been so upset that your only thought was to run away or fight? Describe your experience. What did you do when you were this upset? From what you know about recovery and the brain, how would you have liked to be able to handle the experience?

12. What happens when fear-based thinking dominates us?

13. In your own words, how would you describe dissociation? Why does it happen?

14. Why can positive feelings or euphoric recall be traumatic for the brain?

15. How can Thriving help you heal and grow through the pain of Trauma A and Trauma B?

16. What did you experience during this week's Immanuel Process exercise?

TRAUMA, HOPE AND RECOVERY
TRAUMA

1. Why is recovery from trauma so essential for recovery from BEEPS?

2. How can the Twelve Steps help you to recover from the pain of trauma and attachments to BEEPS?

3. How can dismissive, distracted and disorganized attachment keep you stuck in attachment pain and the BEEPS cycle? Explain.

4. How is the heart that Jesus gave you different from the painful identity that has kept you stuck in trauma and attachments to BEEPS?

5. How have Trauma A and/or Trauma B kept you stuck in cycles of pain that influence your attachments to BEEPS?

6. When we are overwhelmed, communication between the left and right hemispheres of the brain is disrupted. How can this lead to relapse?

7. In recovery, many of us have developed good left-brained relapse prevention plans and thought a lot about how we could avoid using BEEPS. We developed strategies like making phone calls, praying or going to meetings so that we'd know what to do if we felt like using BEEPS. Then, we got so stressed or upset that we used BEEPS anyway, and barely even thought about the plan until later. Has this ever happened to you? Describe this situation. How might this have been different if you had more capacity?

8. Feeling anxious is usually an indication that we are afraid. How do you handle anxiety? What happens to you when your anxiety grows? Have you ever used BEEPS to medicate anxiety? Describe.

9. How do you handle feelings of anger or rage? What happens to you when anger and resentments build? Have you ever used BEEPS as a result? Describe.

10. Can avoiding anxiety and anger work as an effective relapse strategy? From what you have learned in Restarting, what do you need to learn to handle emotions like fear and anger? Where can you find these resources?

11. Have you ever felt like you "just checked out" before you used BEEPS? Describe this experience. What were you feeling before you "checked out?"

12. Why do you think that relapse prevention strategies that focus primarily on the left-brain tend to fail? Why does right-brain training and the development of capacity need to be a part of your recovery?

13. What is euphoric recall? How has euphoric recall been a part of your attachment to BEEPS? What do you need to overcome euphoric recall?

TRAUMA, HOPE AND RECOVERY
TRAUMA

14. How can intense positive emotions contribute to relapse? Has this ever happened to you? Explain.

15. Why do you need a joyful and healing community to recover from the pain of trauma and attachments to BEEPS?

16. What did you experience during this week's Immanuel Process exercise? Do you think that the Immanuel Process can be a helpful part of your recovery program?

9 LEAVING CODEPENDENCY BEHIND
BEEPS MEDICATE TO REGULATE PART 1: SECURE ATTACHMENTS, IDENTITY AND INTERDEPENDENCE

OPEN THE GROUP WITH PRAYER

YOUR NOTES

EXERCISE: A MOMENT WITH JESUS *5 Minutes*

1. Everyone can remain together in a large group for this exercise.

2. Your facilitator will share for one minute about a moment in the past week when he/she experienced the presence of Jesus. Your facilitator will describe that moment and what emotions he/she felt when he/she realized that Jesus was with him/her.

3. Your facilitator will ask volunteers to share about a moment in the past week when they experienced the presence of Jesus.

4. Volunteers each have one minute to share about that moment, and describe the experience and emotions they felt when they realized that Jesus was with them.

5. Your facilitator will help you by keeping track of time.

TODAY'S LESSON: BEEPS Medicate to Regulate Part 1:
Secure Attachments, Identity and Interdependence

CLASS NOTES: Secure Attachments, Identity and Interdependence.

BEEPS
- BEEPS are attachments to Behaviors, Events, Experiences, People or Substances that are used to regulate emotions, increase pleasure or decrease pain.
- Attachments to BEEPS help us medicate – to artificially regulate – positive and negative emotions as well as pain.
- Attachments to BEEPS take the place of secure attachments to God and significant others.

Attachment can lead to:
- Healthy interdependence or
- Harmful dependency.

Thriving is unique:
- The same mechanism that causes us to attach to BEEPS is the same mechanism that helps us securely attach in joyful relationships with God and others.
- Thriving deals with more than negative attachments and the drive to "medicate to regulate."

LEAVING CODEPENDENCY BEHIND
BEEPS MEDICATE TO REGULATE PART 1: SECURE ATTACHMENTS, IDENTITY AND INTERDEPENDENCE

- Thriving teaches us to give our brain what it really wants and really craves, and that is joy – and joyful relationships with others.
- Joy means relationship.

How do we build a strong, joyful identity, healthy attachments and interdependent relationships?

We are created for secure attachments with God and others.
- Everything about us is created to be relational.

Adam and Eve were created for secure attachment and healthy interdependence.
- Let us make man in our own image, in our likeness…So God created man in his own image, in the image of God he created him; male and female he created them. Genesis 1:26, 27, NKJV
- It is not good for the man to be alone. I will make a helper suitable for him...and He brought her to the man. The man said, "This is now flesh of my flesh…For this reason, a man will leave his father and mother and be united to his wife and they will become one flesh." Genesis 2:18, 22, 23, NKJV

Rhythms of joy and quiet together create secure attachment and identity that is joyful, secure and strong.

High joy capacity helps build a strong identity.
- Increasing capacity helps develop an identity that is strong – even when facing distress.

When others are glad to be with me when I am distressed:
- I can learn to return to joy from negative emotions.
- My attachments and bonds remain secure.
- I can act like myself, even when I'm upset.
- These allow secure attachments to grow, even when I'm distressed or upset.
- My individual and group identities are also strengthened.

Secure attachments with a strong, joyful individual and group identity build healthy interdependence.
- Two are better than one, because they have a good return for their work. If one falls down, his friend can help him up. But pity the man who falls and has no one to help him up! Also, if two lie down together they will keep warm. But how can one keep warm alone? Though one may be overpowered, two can defend themselves. A cord of three strands is not easily broken. Ecc. 4:10-12, NIV.

What do healthy attachments and interdependence look like?

Attachment strength: the strength of attachments to BEEPS are reflected by:
- Intensity:
  - How strongly the BEEPS changes emotions, pleasure and/or pain.

LEAVING CODEPENDENCY BEHIND
BEEPS MEDICATE TO REGULATE PART 1: SECURE ATTACHMENTS, IDENTITY AND INTERDEPENDENCE

- Intimacy:
  - How strongly we relate to and rely on BEEPS to medicate emotions, pain and pleasure.
- Exclusivity:
  - The degree to which we focus our time, effort and energy on BEEPS – to the exclusion of other people, things or God.

Healthy attachment strength
- Intensity
  - Attachment center functioning -secure attachment
  - Joyful capacity
  - Value systems
  - Control center well regulated
- Intimacy
  - Growing attachment and synchronization
  - Continue to regulate emotions well
  - Joy builds
  - Anticipate joy at reunion
  - Acquired value
- Exclusivity
  - Growing attachment and synchronization
  - Bond together for life
  - Give and receive life appropriately
  - Maintain other important relationships
- Interdependence
  - Increased maturity and capacity
  - Increased synchronization, mutual mind
  - Open to receive from others – but bonded relationship is primary
  - Family forms

Healthy interdependence: married and singles:
- Both married and singles can form strong bonds that are intense, intimate, and exclusive – and lead to healthy interdependence.
- Both married and singles can form bonds for life that are intense, intimate and exclusive with parents, siblings, extended family, spiritual family and friends.
- The primary differences are the degree of exclusivity and sexual nature of the bonds between married couples.

Intensity
- Something about the other person gets your attention.
- Something says "pay attention to him/her."
- Something feels good about being with them.
- It is fun!

Intimacy
- As the relationship grows, you spend more time together.
- You share friends and friendships together.
- It is fun to be together.
- The relationship grows increasingly close.

LEAVING CODEPENDENCY BEHIND
BEEPS MEDICATE TO REGULATE PART 1: SECURE ATTACHMENTS, IDENTITY AND INTERDEPENDENCE

Intimacy
- Your attachment center lights up when you are with them or think about them.
- You are able to regulate emotions, pleasure and pain independently, but are synchronizing with the other person.
- Love grows until you know that you want to spend the rest of your life in relationship with them.

Exclusivity
- The relationship reaches a level in which your bond is exclusive.
- The relationship you have with your bonded partner, parent, child, sibling, spouse or friend is reserved for only one person – them!
- When your attachment is exclusive and healthy, interdependence helps your bonds grow and mature.

A secure, joyful identity leads to secure and interdependent adult attachments.

What does healthy interdependence feel like? What does healthy interdependence look like?
- Pause for a Level 4+ Healthy Interdependence Story
- Pause for a Level 4 Healthy Interdependence Story

EXERCISE: TELLING LEVEL 4+ AND LEVEL 4 HEALTHY INTERDEPENDENCE STORIES *35 Minutes*

Exercise Part 1: 4+ Stories About Healthy Interdependence *(30 Minutes)*

1. Break into small groups of 3 people.

2. Please locate your "Preparing My 4 + Healthy Interdependence Story Worksheet" in your workbook. In the first part of this exercise, you will tell a story about a relationship you have had that is characterized by healthy interdependence. Your facilitator will review the characteristics of a Level 4+ story with you. (5 Minutes).

   a. Please make sure that your story is not so emotionally intense that it overwhelms others.

   b. It helps if this is a story that you have told before – this makes it easier to share.

   c. It is a good idea to avoid stories that may cause you or others feelings of shame or embarrassment.

   d. Make sure that the story is about your feelings and that you are involved in the story.

   e. Be sure that your story clearly illustrates a specific feeling.

   f. As you tell your story, let your face and voice reflect the emotion you are describing.

   g. As you maintain eye contact with others in your small group, it

LEAVING CODEPENDENCY BEHIND
BEEPS MEDICATE TO REGULATE PART 1: SECURE ATTACHMENTS, IDENTITY AND INTERDEPENDENCE

will help you stay connected relationally with them.

h. Write a brief description of the situation you want to share. You only need to write down enough details to help you remember the story – and be able to share it.

i. Write the feeling words that describe the emotions that you felt during the story. It helps to list each one.

j. Write down how your body felt during the situation you are describing. It may be things like "My stomach was in a knot" or "My shoulders felt tight" or "My muscles felt relaxed."

k. Describe what you did in the story that illustrates how you like to act in a healthy interdependent relationship.

3. Your facilitator will explain how to complete your "Preparing My 4 + Healthy Inter-dependence Story Worksheet."

a. If you have experienced a healthy interdependent relationship, complete your worksheet by describing an event from your relationship.

b. If you have never experienced healthy interdependence, you may describe a healthy interdependent relationship that you have seen between others. Complete your worksheet by describing a time in which you observed this relationship.

c. If you have never seen or experienced a healthy interdependent relationship, you may complete your worksheet and describe what you think this kind of relationship might be like. What emotions do you think you'd feel, what might your body feel like, and how do you think you would act in a healthy interdependent relationship?

4. Your facilitator will tell a 3 minute Level 4+ Healthy Interdependence Story, followed by 2 minutes of feedback. To help you during the feedback session, your facilitator will read each element of a 4+ story listed on the worksheet, and ask you if the story contained each element. Remember that feedback:

a. Is based on helping a storyteller determine if their story contained all the elements of a 4+ story listed on the worksheet.

b. Is not based on criticism or advice about the experience or feelings described.

5. Take 5 minutes to complete your Level 4+ story worksheet. Your facilitator will assist you by keeping track of time, and will let you know when volunteers may begin sharing their stories with their small group.

6. Your facilitator will ask for volunteers in each small group to begin telling their story. You will have 3 minutes to tell your story and your facilitator will keep track of time for you. If at any point your group is stuck or has a question, please raise your hand, and your facilitator will come help you.

PREPARING MY 4+ HEALTHY INTERDEPENDENCE STORY WORKSHEET

1. This story has a moderate feeling level and is not too intense ☐

2. I have told this story before ☐

3. I do not need to be guarded in telling this story ☐

4. This story is autobiographical (I am involved in the story) ☐

5. This story illustrates a specific feeling ☐

6. I will show the authentic emotion on my face and in my voice ☐

7. I will maintain eye contact while storytelling ☐

8. Briefly describe the situation:

9. Feeling words for this story:

10. During this story my body felt:

11. The things I did in this story that demonstrate how I like to act in a healthy interdependence relationship. (or if I did not act like myself at the time, it would have been like me to do this...)

LEAVING CODEPENDENCY BEHIND
BEEPS MEDICATE TO REGULATE PART 1: SECURE ATTACHMENTS, IDENTITY AND INTERDEPENDENCE

7. After the first story, each group can take 2 minutes to give feedback on the story. Use the "Preparing My 4 + Healthy Interdependence Story Worksheet" as a guideline to help the storyteller discover if they were able to share all the elements of a 4+ story listed on the worksheet. Be encouraging and positive! Your facilitator will keep track of time for you, and let you know when it is time for the next person to share their story.

8. Your facilitator will let you know when it is time for a second person in each small group to begin their 3-minute Level 4+ Healthy Interdependence Story, followed by 2 minutes of feedback. Your facilitator will keep track of time for you and let you know when it is time for the next person to share their story.

9. Your facilitator will let you know when it is time for the third person in each small group to begin their 3-minute Level 4+ Healthy Interdependence Story, followed by 2 minutes of feedback. Your facilitator will keep track of time for you.

Exercise Part 2: Level 4 Stories About Healthy Interdependence *(5 Minutes)*

1. You may remain in your small groups as your facilitator reviews the characteristics of Level 4 stories with you.
   a. Level 4 stories are non-verbal stories told without using words.
   b. Level 4 stories rely on the right hemisphere of the brain to describe a feeling, experience, sensation, event or story.
   c. In Level 4 stories, participants act out the story and emotions they are describing using only facial expression, body language, movement or non-verbal interactions with others.

2. Your facilitator will tell a Level 4 Healthy Interdependence Story for the entire group that illustrates what healthy interdependence looks like.

3. Volunteers have the opportunity to tell Level 4 Healthy Interdependence Stories to the entire group.
   a. Remember to tell these stories using only facial expression, body language, movement or non-verbal interactions with others.
   b. Your Level 4 stories can illustrate the experience you described on your Level 4+ worksheet, or they can be spontaneous depictions of healthy interdependence.
   c. Have fun with this! You are, "Going to Hollywood."

4. Your facilitator will keep track of time for you, and will let you know when it is time to restart the video.

LEAVING CODEPENDENCY BEHIND
BEEPS MEDICATE TO REGULATE PART 1: SECURE ATTACHMENTS, IDENTITY AND INTERDEPENDENCE

What happens to my identity and attachments when my capacity for joy is low and I can't effectively regulate negative emotions?

Life is pain-centered, and this makes relationships and attachment difficult.
- When my level of pain exceeds my level of joy, I experience trauma.
- I get stuck in ongoing relational distress and further trauma.
- My attachments and identity are centered in ongoing pain.

When relationships are painful and my personal and group identity is weak, I can't get back to joy and get stuck in:
- Level 1: Attachment pain
- Level 2: Life is bad and scary
- Level 3: Negative emotions
- Level 4: Immaturity
- Level 4+: Inconsistent identity

I will experience ongoing pain and "Medicate to Regulate."

BEEPS
- Attachments to Behaviors, Events, Experiences, People and Substances that are used to regulate emotions, increase pleasure or decrease pain.

BEEPS
- There are many different types of BEEPS. Examples can include:
- Behaviors: Work
- Events: Thrill Seeking
- Experiences: Sex
- People: Relationships
- Substances: Alcohol

BEEPS and Steps 6 and 7
- Step 6: We are entirely ready to have God remove all these defects of character.
- Step 7: Humbly asked Him to remove our shortcomings.

Steps 6 and 7 teach us:
- Life, relationships and recovery thrive when we stop relying on our own limited abilities to change ourselves – but on God who has no limits.
- We cannot change our lives, brains or BEEPS apart from humility and relationship with God
- Change requires the loving involvement of God and others empowered by joy!

My relationships with others can become empowered by joy
- I can be free from attachments to BEEPS
- I can attach to God and to others in joy!

LEAVING CODEPENDENCY BEHIND
BEEPS MEDICATE TO REGULATE PART 1: SECURE ATTACHMENTS, IDENTITY AND INTERDEPENDENCE

EXERCISE: MAGGIE'S STORY *5 Minutes*

1. You can remain in your seats and do not need to break into small groups for this exercise. The purpose of this exercise is to help you describe your feelings after listening to Maggie's story in this week's video.

2. Your facilitator will ask volunteers to share how they feel after watching Maggie's story. Use one or two words to describe your feelings.

CLOSE THE GROUP WITH PRAYER

OPTIONAL EXERCISE: PART 1 - DON'T TALK *20 Minutes*

1. Break into small groups of 3-5 people.

2. In this exercise, you will be using the song "Don't Talk," which describes a conversation between a woman and a man who is drinking too much. The goal of this exercise is to help you apply what you've learned about healthy interdependence to relationships in which BEEPS are involved.

3. Your facilitator may play this song for you – or may read the song lyrics to you.

4. As you listen to the song, pay attention to:
   a. The relationship between the woman and the man.
   b. The impact BEEPS are having on the man who is drinking too much.
   c. The impact of BEEPS upon the woman.

5. When the song is finished, you will have 10 minutes to share the answers to these questions with your group:
   a. What kind of impact are BEEPS having on the man and woman in the song?
   b. What is the difference between their relationship and healthy interdependence?
   c. How are BEEPS keeping them from developing healthy interdependence?

6. Your facilitator will help you by keeping track of time.

7. After 10 minutes of sharing, you may remain in your groups, and your facilitator will lead you in a short relaxation exercise.

LEAVING CODEPENDENCY BEHIND
BEEPS MEDICATE TO REGULATE PART 1: SECURE ATTACHMENTS, IDENTITY AND INTERDEPENDENCE

OPTIONAL EXERCISE: PART 2 - LEARNING TO BREATHE DEEPLY
2 Minutes

1. Follow your facilitator's instructions as you do this exercise.

2. Remain in your small groups. Stand up, and make sure that you have 3-4 feet of clear space around you.

3. Imagine that you are a marionette – a puppet – with a string running from the base of your spine to the top of your head. Imagine that the string is gently pulled upwards and your back, neck and head are perfectly aligned. Your head is at rest and comfortably settled in line with your back and spine. You are looking forward, and your head is settled in comfortably.

4. Bend your knees slightly. You are standing still in a comfortable position.

5. Place your hand over your stomach.

6. Take such a deep breath that you feel your stomach expand as you breathe. Follow your facilitator's instructions as you breathe deeply for a few moments.

7. Your facilitator will keep track of time for you as you relax and breathe deeply.

LEAVING CODEPENDENCY BEHIND
BEEPS MEDICATE TO REGULATE PART 1: SECURE ATTACHMENTS, IDENTITY AND INTERDEPENDENCE

QUESTIONS FOR FURTHER DISCUSSION OR FOLLOW-UP

1. Why is it important for you to know that you are designed for secure attachments and healthy interdependence?

2. What do you need to begin to build an identity that is joyful, secure and strong?

3. We often try to avoid, deny or minimize negative emotions in the mistaken belief that these will always damage or destroy our attachments to others. What really happens to your attachments with others when you try to deny, avoid or minimize negative emotions in your relationship with them? Do our attachments become more – or less secure?

4. What happens to our individual identity and attachments with others when they are glad to be with us when we are experiencing a negative emotion?

5. Why do we need a strong, joyful individual identity to build a healthy group identity?

6. How do you define intensity, intimacy and exclusivity?

7. How can intensity, intimacy and exclusivity describe the strength of your attachments?

8. Have you ever tried to form an attachment with someone – when it didn't feel good to be with them? How did this affect your attachment with them?

9. Why are intensity – and a healthy control center – so important for the development of intimacy in healthy attachments? What happens to intensity if my control center does not function well?

10. How can exclusivity be a healthy part of secure attachment?

11. What characterizes healthy interdependency in relationships? How would you describe it?

12. Can both single and married people develop healthy interdependence in relationships? Why? What is the primary difference between healthy interdependence in the bonds shared in a marriage, and the bonds shared by others?

13. Have you ever been in a relationship with healthy interdependence? Describe your relationship. What was it like? How did it feel? If you have never been in a relationship like this, what do you think it would feel like – and look like?

14. What happens to our identity if our capacity for joy is low, and we tend to get stuck in negative emotions? How does this affect our attachments, and ability to form strong and secure group bonds?

15. Why is it so easy to develop an attachment to BEEPS when our individual and group identity is weak?

16. What do you need to develop a stronger individual group and individual identity? Where are the resources you need?

LEAVING CODEPENDENCY BEHIND
BEEPS MEDICATE TO REGULATE PART 1: SECURE ATTACHMENTS, IDENTITY AND INTERDEPENDENCE

OPTIONAL 12-STEP QUESTIONS

1. In your own words, how would you describe Steps 6 & 7?

2. According to these steps, God is a vital part of our recovery. Why is it so important for God to be involved in helping you overcome your character defects and shortcomings?

3. Do you have character defects that you would like to have God remove? Describe these character defects. How do they affect your life and recovery? Are you entirely ready for Him to remove them?

4. Have you ever asked God to remove a character defect from your life – but then been unwilling to let go of it? What happened? Describe your experience.

5. Are there character defects you are not entirely ready to have God remove? Why are you holding on to them? What do you need to release them?

6. How do you define healthy interdependence? How have your attachments to BEEPS interfered with your ability to form healthy interdependence with others?

7. Have you ever experienced healthy interdependence in a relationship? Describe this relationship. What was it like? How did it feel? If you have never been in a relationship like this, what do you think it would feel like – and look like?

8. How do you answer the question, "Who am I?" How do you describe yourself?

9. Do you think that most of your relationships are rooted in joy – or pain? Why?

10. Who are the people that you like to spend time with the most? Do these relationships help make your identity and bonds stronger – or weaker? Explain.

11. What does the word "shortcomings" mean to you? Can "shortcomings" include things like weak attachments, not knowing how to develop healthy relationships and a painful personal and group identity?

12. What are the shortcomings that you would most like God to remove from you? How do you "humbly" ask God to remove your shortcomings? Write down what you would say.

13. What do you think will happen if you humbly ask God to remove your shortcomings? How long will it take Him to remove them?

14. Asking God to remove your shortcomings also means that you would like God to fill you with new and good things. What gifts would you like to receive from God to replace your shortcomings? Be specific!

15. Would you like to ask God to remove your shortcomings? Explain.

10 ATTACHMENTS THAT KILL: HOW ADDICTIONS REWIRE YOUR BRAIN
BEEPS ATTACHMENT AND IDENTITY - MEDICATE TO REGULATE PART 2: HARMFUL DEPENDENCY

OPEN THE GROUP WITH PRAYER

YOUR NOTES

EXERCISE: APPRECIATION AND HEALTHY INTERDEPENDENCE *10 Minutes*

1. Break into small groups of 3 people.

2. Your facilitator will ask you to think about a moment from the past week in which you had either:
   a. An experience with God or another person for which you are grateful.
   b. An experience of healthy interdependence in your relationship with God or another person for which you are grateful.

3. Your facilitator will share his/her own appreciation moment from the past week with the entire group. While sharing, your facilitator will:
   a. Maintain eye contact.
   b. Identify the experience for which he/she is grateful.
   c. Describe the emotions he/she felt during the experience.
   d. Describe what his/her body felt like during the experience.

4. Your facilitator will ask volunteers to take turns sharing about their own experience with their small group. Each volunteer will have 2 minutes to share. Remember to:
   a. Maintain eye contact while sharing.
   b. Identify the person and experience for which you are grateful.
   c. Describe what emotions you felt during your experience.
   d. Describe what your body felt during that experience.

5. Your facilitator will help you by keeping track of time.

6. When each group is finished, your facilitator may ask volunteers how they feel after the exercise with the entire group. Use one or two words to describe your feelings.

TODAY´S LESSON: BEEPS, Attachment and Identity: Medicate to Regulate Part 2: Harmful Dependency

CLASS NOTES: BEEPS, Attachment & Identity: Medicate to Regulate Part 2: Harmful Dependency

ATTACHMENTS THAT KILL: HOW ADDICTIONS RE-WIRE YOUR BRAIN

BEEPS ATTACHMENT & IDENTITY - MEDICATE TO REGULATE PART 2: HARMFUL DEPENDENCY

BEEPS
- BEEPS are attachments to Behaviors, Events, Experiences, People or Substances that are used to regulate emotions, increase pleasure or decrease pain.
- Attachments to BEEPS help us medicate – to artificially regulate – positive and negative emotions as well as pain.
- Attachments to BEEPS take the place of secure attachments to God and significant others.

Attachment to BEEPS is not about an identity rooted in addiction.
- Attachments to BEEPS result when an identity is rooted in pain.
- When there is no way to effectively regulate pain, pleasure or emotions; BEEPS attachments hijack the attachment center – and lead to harmful dependency.

Attachment can lead to:
- Healthy interdependence or
- Harmful dependency.

How do attachments to BEEPS develop? How does harmful dependency build?

How do BEEPS attachments develop?
- Now the Lord God had planted a garden in the east, in Eden; ("Eden" means "Pleasure") and there he put the man he had formed. And the Lord God made all kinds of trees grow out of the ground – trees that were pleasing to the eye and good for food.
  Genesis 2:8-9. NIV, parenthesis added.
- We are created to experience and enjoy pleasure!

Adam and Eve used Eden to cover and hide from pain.
- Then the eyes of both of them were opened, and they realized they were naked; so they sewed fig leaves together and made coverings for themselves. Then the man and his wife heard the sound of the Lord God as He was walking in the garden in the cool of the day and they hid from the Lord God among the trees of the garden.
  Genesis 3:7-8, NKJV

Adam and Eve used Eden to cover up and hide from:
- God
- Each other
- Painful emotions

They blamed God and each other for their attachment pain (separation from God and each other) and for their ongoing emotional distress.

Broken attachments to God and each other overwhelmed their capacity to handle pain.
- Their level of pain exceeded their level of joy.
- They experienced ongoing relational distress and trauma.
- The greater the attachment pain, the less capacity we have for life.

ATTACHMENTS THAT KILL: HOW ADDICTIONS RE-WIRE YOUR BRAIN
BEEPS ATTACHMENT & IDENTITY - MEDICATE TO REGULATE PART 2: HARMFUL DEPENDENCY

As capacity drops, life becomes more painful.
- I am less able to attach to others in healthy relationships.
- I am stuck in increasing levels of pain.

When I lack joy capacity and get stuck in negative emotions, my attachments with others are a source of ongoing pain.
- Dismissive attachment
- Distracted attachment
- Disorganized attachment

Unresolved attachment pain further diminishes capacity and increases distress:
- Non-secure attachments lead to even greater levels of attachment pain.
- Increasing attachment pain leads to reduced joyful capacity and escalating levels of trauma and chronic distress.
- Rising levels of trauma and chronic distress lead to the development of an identity that is painful.
- My identity is now pain centered.
- I am driven to find relief.

Non-secure attachments and weak identity are the result of:
- Lack of joy capacity.
- Lack of synchronization.
- Getting stuck in pain without the ability to return to joy.
- Level 1 attachment pain.
- An identity that is rooted in pain leads to harmful dependency.

Medicate to regulate

BEEPS
- There are many different types of BEEPS. Examples can include:
- Behaviors: Work
- Events: Thrill Seeking
- Experiences: Sex
- People: Relationships
- Substances: Alcohol

BEEPS hijack the attachment center.
- What we attach to steers us.
- When the emotional control center is hijacked, BEEPS are behind the wheel.
- BEEPS drive us to places of even greater attachment pain.
- BEEPS destroy our lives, homes and relationships.

Attachment strength: the strength of attachments to BEEPS are reflected by:
- Intensity:
  - How strongly the BEEPS changes emotions, pleasure and/or pain.
- Intimacy:
  - How strongly we relate to and rely on BEEPS to medicate emotions, pain and pleasure.

ATTACHMENTS THAT KILL: HOW ADDICTIONS RE-WIRE YOUR BRAIN
BEEPS ATTACHMENT & IDENTITY - MEDICATE TO REGULATE PART 2: HARMFUL DEPENDENCY

- Exclusivity:
  - The degree to which we focus our time, effort and energy on BEEPS – to the exclusion of other people, things or God.

BEEPS attachment strength
The development of an attachment to BEEPS through the stages of intensity, intimacy and exclusivity describes the process by which BEEPS hijack the emotional control center of the brain.
- Intensity:
  - Attachment center and the three non-secure attachment styles
  - Trauma
  - Value systems
  - Control center dysfunction
- Intimacy:
  - Growing BEEPS attachment to regulate emotion, pleasure and pain
  - Implicit memory (euphoric recall)
  - Acquired value
- Exclusivity:
  - Alterations in dopamine receptors
  - Craving
  - Resistant to other attachments and stimuli
  - Structural changes in the control center
- Harmful dependency:
  - Tolerance and withdrawal
  - Relationship destruction
  - Specific BEEPS disease process
  - Increasing breakdown of the control center
  - Illness, high risk behaviors
  - Death

Intensity and trauma
- The neurological and behavioral pathways for addictive behaviors are forged during infancy and childhood through repeated exposure to relational trauma. Once the individual discovers that substance use and related behaviors can expedite and mimic the chemical process that leads to immediate relief from psychic pain, the process shifts to a set of maladaptive addictive behaviors.... Addictive behaviors share the same pathways in the brain with trauma-based behaviors.

  Dr. Joel Porter, 2002.
- This same relationship between trauma and addictive behaviors is further illustrated in Dr. Allan Schore's work "Affect Dysregulation and Disorders of the Self."

Intensity, trauma and monkeys:
- After socialization, dominant (untraumatized) monkeys had 20% more volume ratio for D2 dopamine receptors.
- D2 did not predict social order, but predicted cocaine usage.
- Subordinate monkeys self-administered cocaine at higher rates than dominant.

ATTACHMENTS THAT KILL: HOW ADDICTIONS RE-WIRE YOUR BRAIN
BEEPS ATTACHMENT & IDENTITY - MEDICATE TO REGULATE PART 2: HARMFUL DEPENDENCY

- Subordinate monkeys were more sensitive to the reinforcing effects of cocaine than dominant.
- Dominant monkeys were initially protected from the reinforcing effects of cocaine, but over time, they lost the increased volume of dopamine receptors.

Intimacy, acquired value and memory:
- "Associated memories are laid down that change the emotional value of drugs that created deeply ingrained behavioral responses to those cues."

    Laura Helmuth, Science, Nov. 2, 2001, quoting Steve Hyman, Director of the National Institute of Mental Health.

- "Non-conscious memories are more likely to underlie the compulsive aspect of addiction and the cravings that lead to relapse. For instance, the paraphernalia of drug use – crack pipes, syringes, the sound of ice tinkling in a glass full of scotch – can act as cues that induce craving much like the sound of a bell caused Pavlov's dogs to salivate."

    Laura Helmuth, Science, Nov. 2, 2001, quoting Terry Robinson, University of Michigan.

Exclusivity, D2 receptors and monkeys:
- Cocaine use alters D2 receptor functioning.
    - In humans, even after 4 months abstinence. (The study stopped at 4 months, because everyone relapsed!)
    - In monkeys, even after 7 months.
    - Chronic exposure resulted in persistent reductions in D2 receptor densities.
    - In cocaine using monkeys, receptor binding 20% lower. Controls had excellent uptake in basal ganglia.

        Nader and Czoty, "PET Imaging of Dopamine D2 Receptors in Monkey Models of Cocaine Abuse: Genetic Predisposition Versus Environmental Modulation." American Journal of Psychiatry, 162:8, August. 2005.

- Alcoholics have the same issue in the reward pathway.

    Heinz, et al., "Correlation Between Dopamine D2 Receptors in the Ventral Striatum and Central Process of Alcohol Cues and Craving." American Journal of Psychiatry 2004; 161:1783-1789.

Why is D2 reduction important?
- Impairment in dopamine sensitivity means:
    - The person recovering from BEEPS experiences less pleasure in normal life.
    - Other stimuli – even healthy ones – are not as attractive as the BEEPS.
    - Dopamine processing has been altered to respond primarily to BEEPS.

        Franken, I. H. Drug Craving and Addiction: Integrating Psychological and Neuropsychopharmacological Approaches. Prog. Neuropsychopharmocological Biologic Psychiatry. 2003 June; 27(4):563-79.

- This makes the BEEPS relationship even more exclusive.
- **BEEPS is a jealous lover!**

ATTACHMENTS THAT KILL: HOW ADDICTIONS RE-WIRE YOUR BRAIN

BEEPS ATTACHMENT & IDENTITY - MEDICATE TO REGULATE PART 2: HARMFUL DEPENDENCY

YOUR NOTES

Disruption of the control center

The following studies are not discussed on the video, but are included here for your review.

- Numerous studies suggest alterations in the functions of the basal ganglia and thalamus, amygdala, cingulate cortex, and the orbitoprefrontal cortex:
  - "These alterations suggest that during craving, activity in reward pathways increases, while cognitive control decreases."
  - "These may be a consequence of a pre-existent vulnerability to addictive behavior."
    "Substance Use Disorders and the Orbitofrontal Cortex." British Journal of Psychiatry, 2005. 187, 209-220.
- Other studies suggest:
  - Executive dysfunction in the right prefrontal cortex and cingulate and over-reliance on the left hemisphere of the brain to complete tasks.
  - This makes it hard to inhibit behavior.
  - Addiction deregulates executive functioning.
  - Personality changes.
    Hester & Garavan. "Executive Dysfunction in Cocaine Addiction: Evidence for Discordant Frontal, Cingulate and Cerebellar Activity." The Journal of Neuroscience, December 8, 2004. 24(49); 11017-11022.
    Heinz, et al. "Correlation Between Dopamine D2 Receptors in the Ventral Striatum and Central Processing of Alcohol Cues and Craving." American Journal of Psychiatry 2004; 161:1783-1789.

Since BEEPS are about a painful identity, effective recovery must:

- Be relational.
- Recognize and identify both beeps and pain.
- Address both BEEPS and the painful identity.
- Develop secure relationships with others that are empowered by joy.
- Change my identity!

Sobriety is the primary focus of self-help and Twelve Step recovery groups.

- Helping participants remain abstinent from life-controlling and destructive addictions is the primary goal of most Twelve Step and self-help groups.
- Since addictions destroy lives, family and relationships, sobriety is essential.
- The Twelve Steps can help provide an important blueprint for sobriety.

The goals of Thriving are deeper:

- Thriving is a relational program that is based on cutting-edge research from "The Decade of the Brain."
- Thriving teaches participants the joy and relationship-building skills they need to help the brain heal from the devastating effects of unhealthy attachments and traumas.
- Thriving promotes sobriety – but much, much more.

ATTACHMENTS THAT KILL: HOW ADDICTIONS RE-WIRE YOUR BRAIN
BEEPS ATTACHMENT & IDENTITY - MEDICATE TO REGULATE PART 2: HARMFUL DEPENDENCY

Thriving leads to identity change and the growth of healing community.
- As the brain becomes empowered by joy, Thriving participants are able to connect to others in ways that are mutually life giving.
- A new joyful identity develops that leads to mutually satisfying relationships – and the growth of ongoing maturity.
- Life-giving and joyful community allows all members to grow together.

Thriving and Steps 8 & 9
- Step 8: Made a list of all persons we had harmed, and became willing to make amends to them all.
- Step 9: Made direct amends to such people wherever possible, except when to do so would injure them or others.

BEEPS recovery is about relationship.
- When we are attached to BEEPS, we use people, places and things to regulate pain.
- An essential task for recovery is making amends to others that we have harmed through BEEPS.
- This can help us restore relationships and build healthy attachments with others.

Steps 8 and 9 and identity:
- Accepting responsibility for the harm my BEEPS attachments have caused is only the beginning.
- To change my identity, I must develop and maintain secure and joyful attachments with others.
- Steps 8 & 9 help me develop these new and life-giving relationships.

EXERCISE: TELLING A LEVEL 4 ATTACHMENT TO BEEPS STORY
15 Minutes

1. It is not necessary to break into small groups for this exercise.

2. Your facilitator will review the characteristics of a Level 4 story with you.
   a. Level 4 stories are non-verbal stories.
   b. Level 4 stories express the experiences, feelings, and sensations of the right hemisphere, without using words from the left hemisphere of the brain to describe them.
   c. In Level 4 stories, participants act out the story and emotions they are describing using only facial expression, body language, movement or non-verbal interactions with others.

3. Your facilitator will take a few minutes to talk with you about euphoric recall.
   a. Since this lesson discussed attachments to BEEPS and euphoric

ATTACHMENTS THAT KILL: HOW ADDICTIONS RE-WIRE YOUR BRAIN
BEEPS ATTACHMENT & IDENTITY - MEDICATE TO REGULATE PART 2: HARMFUL DEPENDENCY

recall in detail, it is very normal that some of you may be experiencing euphoric recall about past use of BEEPS.

b. Euphoric recall is a neurochemical process triggered by conscious or sub-concious memories of the pleasure we felt when we used BEEPS.

c. Experiencing euphoric recall is not shameful. Learning to overcome an experience of euphoric recall is a normal part of recovery.

d. Your facilitator will share a Level 4+ story with you about a time in which he/she experienced – and overcame – euphoric recall.

4. When your facilitator's Level 4+ story about euphoric recall is complete, your facilitator will ask volunteers to share one-word descriptions of what attachments to BEEPS feel like.

5. Your facilitator will tell a Level 4 BEEPS Attachment Story for the entire group that describes what BEEPS attachments look like.

6. Volunteers have the opportunity to tell a Level 4 story about what attachments to BEEPS look like.

a. Remember to tell these stories using only facial expression, body language, or movement.

b. Have fun with this! You are, "Going to Hollywood."

7. Your facilitator will help you by keeping track of time.

EXERCISE: RELAXING WITH JESUS - THE IMMANUEL PROCESS
25 Minutes

1. Break into small groups of 3-5 people.

2. For the first part of this exercise, you are welcome to find a comfortable position in which you can rest and relax. You may remain in your chair, sit or lie down on the floor, stand – or whatever feels most comfortable to you. (5-7 Minutes)

3. Place your hand over your stomach. Take such a deep breath that you feel your stomach expand as you breathe. Follow your facilitator's instructions as you breathe deeply for a few moments.

a. When we are stressed, we tend to take rapid shallow breaths. By learning deep breathing exercises and paying attention to what our bodies are doing, we are making sure that our brain is receiving enough oxygen, and we are activating the right orbital prefrontal cortex of our brain.

b. Practicing deep breathing exercises can also help us think through our options when we are distressed, and avoid making poor decisions made in hasty reactions to stress.

ATTACHMENTS THAT KILL: HOW ADDICTIONS RE-WIRE YOUR BRAIN
BEEPS ATTACHMENT & IDENTITY - MEDICATE TO REGULATE PART 2: HARMFUL DEPENDENCY

c. Both of these are helpful in overcoming cravings and BEEPS attachments. They can also help us to relax and improve our ability to perceive the presence of Jesus with us.

4. As you continue to breathe deeply and relax, your facilitator will share with you a time when he/she experienced the presence of God in a way that was meaningful and memorable. He/she will describe:

a. What happened in the experience he/she is describing.

b. The emotions he/she felt when he/she was with Jesus.

c. What his/her body felt like when he/she was with Jesus.

d. What he/she did when he/she experienced His presence.

5. When the story is complete, your facilitator will remind you to continue to breathe deeply.

6. Your facilitator will also explain the reasons that some people may have difficulty experiencing or perceiving the presence of Jesus. (2 Minutes)

a. Some participants may not be able to describe a "peak experience" or time in which they felt particularly close with Jesus. This may be due to a variety of factors, including the presence of exceptionally severe trauma that has formed blockages that keep them from perceiving His presence. These participants can be encouraged that Jesus often wants to help them by bringing other people into their life that can help them resolve these blockages.

b. Some may have never asked Jesus to be part of their life, and as a result, have had no real awareness of His presence. It may be appropriate to ask these participants if they would like to invite Jesus to help them perceive His presence.

c. Some participants may experience strong fear that keeps them from perceiving Jesus' presence – or may never have learned to recognize the presence of Jesus.

d. All participants – regardless of their ability to perceive the presence of Jesus – are encouraged to continue with their deep breathing and relaxation exercises throughout the entire exercise. They are also invited to participate in the entire Immanuel Process exercise to whatever extent they feel comfortable.

7. Your facilitator will again remind you to continue to breathe deeply.

8. Your facilitator will invite you to close your eyes, and ask Jesus to help you remember a time when you felt very close to Him. As your eyes are closed, your facilitator may help you by quietly asking the questions listed below. You do not need to answer these questions aloud; the questions are only to help you focus on the memory of your experience with Jesus. Your facilitator will help you by keeping track of time during this portion of the exercise and let you know when it is time to open your eyes. (3 Minutes)

ATTACHMENTS THAT KILL: HOW ADDICTIONS RE-WIRE YOUR BRAIN

BEEPS ATTACHMENT & IDENTITY - MEDICATE TO REGULATE PART 2: HARMFUL DEPENDENCY

    a. What is happening in the experience you are remembering?

    b. What emotions are you feeling?

    c. What does your body feel like when you are with Jesus?

    d. What are you doing in that memory?

    e. How does it feel to be with Jesus?

9. After you have had the time to reflect on this experience with Jesus, you may ask Jesus a series of questions. As before, your facilitator may help you by quietly reminding you of these questions. You do not need to answer these questions aloud. You may ask these questions silently, and wait to perceive a response. These can include questions like: (3 Minutes)

    a. Jesus, do you love me?

    b. Are you glad to be with me?

    c. Is there anything you would like to say to me now?

    d. Is there anything you want me to do now?

10. Your facilitator will help you by keeping track of time during this portion of the exercise, and let you know when it is time to open your eyes.

11. After you open your eyes, please gather in your small groups, and volunteers can begin to take turns sharing about their experience for 2 minutes. Your facilitator will help you keep track of time as you share. Remember to stay relational by making eye contact as you describe:

    a. The experience with Jesus you just remembered.

    b. The emotions you felt in the memory.

    c. What your body felt like.

    d. What you did when you felt the presence of Jesus.

    e. How it feels to remember this experience with Jesus.

12. When each participant has had the opportunity to share their experience with their small group, your facilitator may ask volunteers to describe what it feels like to experience the presence of Jesus with the entire group. Use one or two words to describe your feelings. (1-2 Minutes)

CLOSE THE GROUP WITH PRAYER

ATTACHMENTS THAT KILL: HOW ADDICTIONS RE-WIRE YOUR BRAIN
BEEPS ATTACHMENT & IDENTITY - MEDICATE TO REGULATE PART 2: HARMFUL DEPENDENCY

QUESTIONS FOR FURTHER DISCUSSION OR FOLLOW-UP

1. How can covering up, hiding or denial of our problems lead to attachment pain? How has your own covering, hiding and denial increased your level of attachment pain?

2. Have you ever blamed other people, places or things for problems and pain that are your own responsibility? Have you ever blamed these people, places or things for your own attachments to BEEPS? Explain.

3. Do you believe that a significant portion of your identity has been pain-centered? Explain. How has this affected your life?

4. Have attachments to BEEPS taken your life to places of even greater pain? What happened? List at least 3 of these painful places.

5. What is the intensity stage of attachments to BEEPS? Why is intensity so important in the development of attachments to BEEPS?

6. Why is it so easy for BEEPS to feel so intensely pleasurable when our control center is not functioning effectively?

7. How do you define the intimacy stage of attachment to BEEPS? How does this lead to stronger attachments to BEEPS?

8. What is euphoric recall? Why is it such an important part of the development of attachment to BEEPS? Why is it so important in relapse? Has it ever been a part of your own BEEPS relapse?

9. What is acquired value? Why do things associated with our use of BEEPS become important relapse triggers?

10. How do you define the exclusivity stage of attachments to BEEPS?

11. What is craving? Why are BEEPS such a jealous lover?

12. What are the characteristics of the harmful dependency stage of attachments to BEEPS?

13. Why is it essential for you to have a change of identity in recovery?

14. List 5 essential characteristics of an effective trauma and BEEPS recovery program.

15. Why do you need a joyful recovery community? Where is your own joyful recovery community?

16. Why are Steps 8 and 9 important for relational recovery?

17. Describe your experience with the Immanuel Process exercise this week.

ATTACHMENTS THAT KILL: HOW ADDICTIONS RE-WIRE YOUR BRAIN
BEEPS ATTACHMENT & IDENTITY - MEDICATE TO REGULATE PART 2: HARMFUL DEPENDENCY

OPTIONAL 12-STEP QUESTIONS

1. What do Steps 8 and 9, and the word "amends" mean to you? Why are these important for your recovery?

2. Has your identity become largely rooted in pain? List 3 characteristics of your painful identity that you would like to change in recovery.

3. Denying, covering up or hiding our problems and attachments to BEEPS – and blaming them on other people, places and things – are characteristics of an identity that is rooted in pain.
   a. Make a list of as many problems and attachments to BEEPS that you tried to cover up, hide or deny as you can recall. How did you try to hide, cover up or deny these issues? Be as specific as you can.
   b. Make a list of as many people, places and things you blamed for your problems and attachments to BEEPS as you can recall. What problems did you blame on each of these? Be as specific as you can.

4. Did covering up, hiding, denial and blaming increase your own level of attachment pain? How did you handle this increased pain?

5. Who were the people that were affected by the hiding, covering up, denial and blaming that you listed in question 3? How did your actions affect each of them? Be specific.

6. As our attachments with BEEPS became more intimate and exclusive, we had less time, attention, effort and resources for relationships with those who cared about us the most. Make a list of the people who were most affected as our time, attention, effort and resources became increasingly devoted to BEEPS. Describe how your attachments to BEEPS affected each one. Be specific.

7. Are there other people that your attachments to BEEPS harmed that you have not listed yet? Who are these people, and how did your BEEPS attachments hurt them?

8. Why is it so important to make amends to those we have harmed?

9. Are you willing to make amends to the people you've harmed?
   a. Make a list of the people you've harmed and to whom you are willing to make amends. List the specific amends you would like to make.
   b. Make a list of the people you've harmed – but to whom you don't want to make amends. What do you need to become willing?

10. Step 9 says that whenever possible, we should make direct amends to all those we've harmed – except when to do so would injure them or others. Are there people on your list that would be harmed if you tried to make amends?

11. How can a joyful community help you develop a new identity – and build the capacity to make amends to others?

12. What are the 5 characteristics of an effective recovery program?

13. Why do you need a joyful community to recover from trauma and attachments to BEEPS?

14. What resources do you need to help you work on Steps 8 and 9? What are they, and where can you find them?

11 RECOVERING OUR LOST IDENTITY
MATURITY AND CAPACITY PART 1: WHAT IS MATURITY?

EXERCISE: A NEW BEGINNING *10 Minutes*

1. Break into small groups of 3-5 people.

2. Your facilitator will share with you that:

   a. Recovery is a journey in which we are empowered to discover a new life – and recover our true identity.

   b. It is a journey of hope, and a new beginning.

   c. It is important to begin to think about what our new life in recovery can be like.

3. Your facilitator will share with you either:

   a. Three characteristics that describe what their life is like now that they are in recovery.

   b. Three characteristics that describe what they hope their life will be like in recovery.

4. Your facilitator will ask you the question, "What do you want your life in recovery to look like?" Take a few minutes to ask yourself this question, and then write down three things that you hope will characterize your new life in recovery.

Characteristic 1: _____

Characteristic 2: _____

Characteristic 3: _____

5. Your facilitator will let you know when volunteers can begin sharing their answers with their small group. You will each have 2 minutes to share.

   a. Remember to make eye contact as you share your answers.

   b. Remember to listen as each person shares, and do not offer feedback or advice.

6. Your facilitator will help you by keeping track of time for you.

TODAY´S LESSON: Maturity and Capacity Part 1: What is Maturity?

CLASS NOTES: Maturity and Capacity Part 1: What is Maturity?

RECOVERING OUR LOST IDENTITY
MATURITY AND CAPACITY PART 1: WHAT IS MATURITY?

So what is maturity?
- What does it look like?
- How do you know it when you see it?

Growth and maturity are God's ideas!
- Then God blessed them, and God said to them, "Be fruitful and multiply; fill the earth and subdue it..." Genesis 1:28, NKJV

He created us to need others to grow into full maturity.
- Without others, it is impossible for us to mature.

We are not born fully mature, physically or spiritually

Maturity is a lifetime journey:
- Until we're all moving rhythmically and easily with each other, efficient and graceful in response to God's Son, fully mature adults, fully developed without and within, fully alive like Christ.
    Ephesians 4:11-13 The Message.

Maturity is not based on physical age.

Physical age is relevant
- But not the only determining factor for defining maturity.

A five year old cannot be an elder
- Although a fifty year old can be stuck at an infant level of maturity.

Maturing means reaching our God given potential.

We mature when we maximize our identity.

We use our skills and talents effectively.

Maturity is growing to the full capacity of our individual designs.

Maturity is not a spiritual gift nor is it a by-product of salvation.

Maturity does not fall from heaven.
- Maturity is a gift we give each other.

Maturity does not grow on trees.
- We grow maturity ourselves through hard work.

Maturity is the human task:
- Redemption is God's task:
    - Healing
    - Deliverance
    - Salvation
    - Sanctification

Maturing means we receive before we give.

RECOVERING OUR LOST IDENTITY
MATURITY AND CAPACITY PART 1: WHAT IS MATURITY?

Maturity is something we work on our entire lives.
- Some are just a little further along than others!

Maturing never ends or finishes.
- We never stop needing other people.

Family and community help us mature.

Life in community is best when people have life-giving relationships with those in all the other stages of life.

Maturing doesn't give us more value.
- As for the man who is weak in faith, welcome him, but not for disputes over opinions. One believes he may eat anything, while the weak man eats only vegetables. Let not him who eats despise him who abstains, and let not him who abstains pass judgment on him who eats; for God has welcomed him. Romans 14:1-3, RSV

Maturing is valuable
- And his gifts were that some should be apostles, some prophets, some evangelists, some pastors and teachers, to equip the saints for the work of ministry, for building up the body of Christ, until we all attain to the unity of the faith and of the knowledge of the Son of God, to mature manhood, to the measure of the stature of the fullness of Christ; so that we may no longer be children, tossed to and fro and carried about with every wind of doctrine, by the cunning of men, by their craftiness in deceitful wiles. Rather, speaking the truth in love, we are to grow up in every way into him who is the head, into Christ. Ephesians 4:11-15, RSV.

How do we build capacity and maturity?

Attachments are the building blocks for mature and healthy brains.
- Healthy attachments to others who are empowered by joy create healthy brains that can regulate emotions, pleasure and pain.
- Unhealthy attachments to others who are not empowered by joy create unhealthy brains that do not effectively regulate emotions, pleasure and pain.

Secure attachment results from high joy capacity and synchronized bonds.
- My identity is joyful, strong and secure.
- This allows me to form secure bonds with others.

The brain has two hemispheres that are different:
- Left hemisphere: naming and explaining
- Right hemisphere: knowing and experience

Building joy and joy capacity help build maturity.
- Increasing capacity helps develop identity that is strong – even when facing increasing distress.
- Maturity grows.

RECOVERING OUR LOST IDENTITY
MATURITY AND CAPACITY PART 1: WHAT IS MATURITY?

I mature in rhythms of joy and quiet together that create secure attachments and an identity that is joyful, secure and strong.

When others are glad to be with us when we are distressed:
- I can learn to return to joy from negative emotions.
- My attachments and bonds remain secure.
- I can act like myself, even when I'm upset.
- I learn this skill in the second year of life.
- These allow secure attachments to grow, even when I'm distressed or upset.
- My individual and group identity is strengthened, and this helps me grow in maturity through pain!

Secure attachments with a strong, joyful individual and group identity build healthy interdependence and ongoing maturity.

BEEPS
- Pseudo joy can produce the appearance of capacity and maturity.
- But will fail under stress.

BEEPS and pseudo joy will always result in ongoing and chronic immaturity.

Immaturity is a level 4 problem in the emotional control center.
- BEEPS are the result of a catastrophic failure to reach adult maturity – and keep us stuck in immaturity!

The Twelve Steps can help us address the pain and trauma of the BEEPS cycle:
- Relationship with God
  - Steps 1, 2, 3 and 11.
- Relationship with Self
  - Steps 4, 5, 6, 7 and 10.
- Relationship with Others
  - Steps 8, 9, and 12.
- When these relationships grow in balance, our recovery will also remain balanced.
- Without growth in all 3 of these relationships, recovery will be out of balance, and will not stand.
- Steps 10, 11 & 12 are called "maintenance steps" and can help produce ongoing sobriety & maturity.

Steps 10 – 12: maintaining and maturing
- Step 10: self
  - Continued to take personal inventory and when we were wrong, promptly admitted it.
- Step 11: God
  - Sought through prayer and meditation to improve our conscious contact with God as we understood Him, praying only for the knowledge of His will for us and the power to carry that out.

RECOVERING OUR LOST IDENTITY
MATURITY AND CAPACITY PART 1: WHAT IS MATURITY?

- Step 12: others
  - Having had a spiritual awakening as a result of these steps, we tried to carry this message to alcoholics, and to practice these principles in all our affairs.

EXERCISE: A SCRIPTURE MEDITATION - TALKING TO JESUS *40 Minutes*

1. It is not necessary to break into small groups for the first part of this exercise.

2. Locate the Scripture Meditation Worksheet in your workbook. Listen as your facilitator explains the purpose of this exercise.

   a. This exercise is similar to the Immanuel Process that we have already learned.

   b. The purpose of this exercise is to help you learn to experience the presence of Jesus in a conversation with Him about a passage of scripture.

   c. You will also learn to journal, as you write down the impressions you have during your conversation with Him.

   d. This exercise is not intended to be a traditional Bible study or information gathering exercise that focuses on assimilating new information for the left hemisphere of your brain.

   e. Both hemispheres of the brain are involved as you read the scriptures, experience the presence of Jesus and interact with Him about the scriptures. This leads to spiritual formation and life transformation – not information accumulation.

3. Your facilitator will explain why there are scriptures on your worksheet.

   a. Notice the scripture from Genesis 4:18 on your worksheet. This scripture is listed because it is an example of a scripture that is not a very helpful passage to use for this exercise.

   b. The other scriptures listed on your worksheet are examples of scriptures that are easier to use for this exercise.

4. Your facilitator will review the following directions with you, and then demonstrate the exercise for you. To demonstrate this exercise, your facilitator will:

   a. Find a comfortable position.

   b. Choose a passage of scripture for the worksheet, and read it out loud.

   c. If any particular part of the passage catches his/her attention, your facilitator will stop and ask Jesus aloud what He would like him/her to know about or understand about it.

   d. If nothing in the passage catches his/her attention, your facilitator will wait until he/she has read the entire passage, and then ask Jesus what He would like him/her to know or understand about it. He/she can also ask the questions listed on the worksheet.

RECOVERING OUR LOST IDENTITY
MATURITY AND CAPACITY PART 1: WHAT IS MATURITY?

YOUR NOTES

e. Your facilitator will stop, listen and pay attention to any impression or thought that comes to mind. Your facilitator will report these impressions to you out loud and record them on the worksheet.

f. Your facilitator will continue to dialogue with Jesus about the passage of scripture, ask questions, report impressions to you and write the impressions on the worksheet.

g. Your facilitator will thank Jesus when the dialogue is complete.

5. Your facilitator will explain that because many of us perceive the presence of Jesus in different ways, this exercise emphasizes the "impressions" that we may experience during the exercise.

a. Sometimes we become aware of new thoughts as we dialogue with Him.

b. Sometimes, we may have a new picture in our mind that is based on the scripture or on our conversation with Jesus.

c. Sometimes we may simply sense, feel and know that Jesus is with us.

d. Focus your attention on perceiving His presence and experiencing His responses to you. Be open to Him making His presence known to you in creative and different ways. Record whatever impression of His presence you experience during the exercise.

e. It is not necessary to record our experiences with phrases like, "Thus saith the Lord," or "God says."

6. Your facilitator will ask you to break into small groups of 3-5 people. When you have moved your chairs, please find a position that will be comfortable as you begin the exercise. You are welcome to remain in your seats, sit on the floor, lie down or stand up.

7. Your facilitator will ask you to choose a passage of scripture from the worksheet. Your facilitator will give you the following instructions:

a. Read the passage of scripture silently.

b. If any particular part of the passage catches your attention, stop and silently ask Jesus what He would like you to know about or understand about it.

c. If nothing in the passage catches your attention, wait until you have read the entire passage, and then silently ask Jesus what He would like you to know or understand about it. You can also ask the questions listed on the worksheet.

d. Stop, listen and pay attention to any impression or thought that comes to your mind.

e. Record your impression on your worksheet.

RECOVERING OUR LOST IDENTITY
MATURITY AND CAPACITY PART 1: WHAT IS MATURITY?

    f. Continue your conversation with Jesus about the passage of scripture, and record your impressions on your worksheet.

    g. When you have completed your dialogue, you may thank Jesus – or tell him what you appreciate about your time together.

8. When your facilitator has finished reading these instructions, you may begin your conversation with Jesus. You will have 5-10 minutes for this portion of the exercise. Your facilitator will help you by keeping track of time.

9. Your facilitator will let you know when it is time to begin sharing your impressions in your small group.

    a. Volunteers may take turns sharing their impressions from the exercise. Each person will have 3 minutes to share.

    b. Remember to stay relational by making eye contact as you share.

    c. When a group member is sharing, be supportive to them through active listening. It is not necessary to offer feedback, comments or criticism of their impressions.

    d. Your facilitator will help you by keeping track of time for you.

10. When small group sharing is finished, your facilitator may ask volunteers to share one or two words with the entire group that describe their experience with Jesus.

CLOSE THE GROUP WITH PRAYER

MY SCRIPTURE MEDITATION WORKSHEET

Don't choose a passage of scripture like this to learn this exercise:

> *And unto Enoch was born Irad: and Irad begat Mehujael: and Mehujael begat Methusael: and Methusael begat Lamech. Genesis 4:18, KJV*

Choose one of these passages of scripture for this exercise:

1. *The Lord bless you and keep you; the Lord make his face shine upon you and be gracious to you. The Lord turn his face toward you and give you peace.* Numbers 6:24-26, NIV

   Questions:

   Why do You long to shine your face upon me?

   Why do You want me to know this?

   Why is there peace when Your face is toward me?

MY SCRIPTURE MEDITATION WORKSHEET

2. *Keep your lives free from the love of money and be content with what you have, because God has said, "Never will I leave you; Never will I forsake you." So we say with confidence, "The Lord is my helper; I will not be afraid. What can man do to me?"* Hebrews 13:5-6, NIV

Questions:

What does it mean that You will never leave me?

Why don't I have to be afraid?

What does your help for me look like?

MY SCRIPTURE MEDITATION WORKSHEET

3. *The Lord is my shepherd, I shall lack nothing. He makes me lie down in green pastures, he leads me beside quiet waters, He restores my soul.*
Psalm 23:1-3, NIV

Questions:

Why do I lack nothing when You are with me?

Where are the quiet waters?

How do You want to restore my soul?

RECOVERING OUR LOST IDENTITY
MATURITY AND CAPACITY PART 1: WHAT IS MATURITY?

QUESTIONS FOR FURTHER DISCUSSION OR FOLLOW-UP

1. How do you define maturity? Why is maturity a lifetime journey?

2. What does it mean to you to be "fully alive like Christ?"

3. Why is your level of maturity not solely based on your physical age?

4. What do you think will happen to your individual and group identity as you mature?

5. Why do you need others to mature? Who are the people God has placed in your life to help you mature?

6. What is God's part in helping you mature? What is your part in developing your own maturity? Why is it important for you to know the difference?

7. Why do you need to learn to receive before you can give? Is it harder for you to receive than it is to give? Why?

8. Will you become more valuable as you become more mature? Why?

9. What are pseudo joy and pseudo maturity? Why do these give us the appearance of maturity?

10. Have BEEPS given you a sense of pseudo maturity? How did they do this? Be specific.

11. What happened to your pseudo maturity as stress increased? Be specific.

12. Explain this statement in your own words. "BEEPS are the result of a catastrophic failure to reach adult maturity – and keep us stuck in immaturity."

13. Why are Steps 10, 11 and 12 called "maintenance steps?" How can practicing these steps with a joyful and healing community help us grow and mature?

14. What did you experience in your conversation with Jesus about scripture in this week's exercise?

RECOVERING OUR LOST IDENTITY
MATURITY AND CAPACITY PART 1: WHAT IS MATURITY?

OPTIONAL 12-STEP QUESTIONS

1. Why is maturity an essential part of recovery?

2. Why are Steps 10, 11 and 12 called "maintenance steps?"

3. How can these steps help produce ongoing sobriety and maturity?

4. In your own words, what does Step 10 mean to you?

5. How can you continue to take your own inventory and promptly admit it when you are wrong? What people and resources do you need to help you?

6. What does Step 11 mean to you? Explain.

7. Do you know how to improve your conscious contact with God? Describe.

8. What did you experience in your conversation with Jesus about scripture in this week's exercise?

9. Can talking with Jesus about scripture help you improve your conscious contact with God? How?

10. Why is it important for you to pray for the knowledge of God's will for you, and the power to carry it out?

11. What does Step 12 mean to you?

12. What is a "spiritual awakening?" Have you had a spiritual awakening in recovery? How did this happen?

13. How can you carry the message of recovery to others who are attached to BEEPS? How can you do this now?

14. Would you like to practice Twelve Step and recovery principles in every part of your life? What does this practically mean for your life? Are there areas of your life in which you resist practicing these principles?

12 THE BLUEPRINT FOR A NEW YOU!
MATURITY AND CAPACITY PART 2: THE STAGES OF MATURITY

EXERCISE: APPRECIATION AND MATURITY *10 Minutes*

1. Break into small groups of 3-5 people.

2. Your facilitator will review some of the characteristics of maturity from last week's lesson. It feels life-giving to be with people who are maturing, because they are:
   a. Becoming more fully alive.
   b. Maximizing their unique identity.
   c. Reaching their God-given potential.
   d. Using gifts and skills wisely.

3. Your facilitator will share an appreciation moment about an experience he/she has had with a person in his/her own life who is maturing. While sharing, your facilitator will:
   a. Maintain eye contact.
   b. Identify the person and experience for which they are grateful.
   c. Describe the emotions they felt during the experience.
   d. Describe what their body felt like during the experience.

4. Your facilitator will ask volunteers to take turns sharing about their own experience with a person who is maturing. Each volunteer will have 2 minutes to share. Remember to:
   a. Maintain eye contact while sharing.
   b. Identify the person and experience for which you are grateful.
   c. Describe what emotions you felt during your experience.
   d. Describe what your body felt like during that experience.

5. Your facilitator will help you by keeping track of time.

6. When each group is finished, your facilitator may ask volunteers how they feel after the exercise with the entire group. Use one or two words to describe your feelings.

TODAY´S LESSON: Maturity and Capacity Part 2: The Stages of Maturity

CLASS NOTES: Maturity and Capacity Part 2: The Stages of Maturity

THE BLUEPRINT FOR A NEW YOU!
MATURITY AND CAPACITY PART 2: THE STAGES OF MATURITY

A quick review

Growth and maturity are god's ideas!
- Then God blessed them, and God said to them, "Be fruitful and multiply; fill the earth and subdue it..." Genesis 1:28, NKJV

We are not born fully mature, physically or spiritually.

Maturity is a lifetime journey:
- Until we're all moving rhythmically and easily with each other, efficient and graceful in response to God's Son, fully mature adults, fully developed without and within, fully alive like Christ.

Ephesians 4:11-13. The Message.

What are the stages of maturity?
- Where am I going?
- How will I know when I get there?

Maturity stages
- Unborn: pre-birth
- Infant: birth to 3 years old
- Child: age 4 to 12 years old
- Adult: age 13 to birth of first child
- Parent: until youngest child is 13
- Elder: begins when youngest child becomes an adult

The six stages of maturity consist of tasks and needs to be accomplished at each stage of life.

Unborn: pre-birth
- Grows a working body.

Infant: receives, learns, lives through joy
- Needs:
  - Joy bonds with both parents that are strong, loving, caring, secure
  - Important needs are met without asking
  - Quiet together time
  - Help regulating distress and emotions
  - Be seen through the "eyes of heaven"
  - Receive and give life
  - Have others synchronize with him/her first
- Tasks:
  - Receive with joy
  - Learn to synchronize with others
  - Organize self into a person through imitation
  - Learn to regulate emotions
  - Learn to return to joy from every emotion
  - Learn to be the same person over time
  - Learn self-care skills
  - Learn to rest

THE BLUEPRINT FOR A NEW YOU!
MATURITY AND CAPACITY PART 2: THE STAGES OF MATURITY

Child: develops an individual identity
- Needs:
  - Help to do what he or she does not feel like doing
  - Help sorting feelings, imaginations and reality
  - Feedback on guesses, attempts and failures
  - Be taught the family history
  - Be taught the history of God's family
  - Be taught the "big picture" of life
- Tasks:
  - Take care of self (one is enough for right now)
  - Learn to ask for what she/he needs
  - Self expression
  - Helping others understand you
  - Develop personal resources and talents
  - Learn to do "hard things"
  - Learn what satisfies
  - See self through the "eyes of heaven"

Adult: develops a group identity
- Needs
  - Time with peers to form a group identity
  - Inclusion in their same-gender community
  - Participation with same-gender leaders who use power fairly and well
  - Be given important tasks by their community
  - Feedback on their personal impact on history
  - Opportunities to share in life partnership
- Tasks
  - Take care of two or more at the same time
  - Discover the main characteristics of his heart
  - Bring self and others back to joy simultaneously
  - Develop a personal style that reflects her heart
  - Learn to protect others from himself or herself
  - Learn mutual satisfaction
  - Diversify and blend roles
  - Learn to express life-giving sexuality
  - Partnership

Young adults: the power years
- Power, relationships and truth are the three preoccupations of young adults.
- Particular attention must be given to their proper development during the "power years" of a young adult's life.

Young adults: power
- Observe adults using power wisely
- Do important tasks for her/his community
- Make an impact on history
- Learn significant roles
- Use sexual power wisely
- Protect others from himself/herself

THE BLUEPRINT FOR A NEW YOU!
MATURITY AND CAPACITY PART 2: THE STAGES OF MATURITY

Young adults: relationships
- Bond with peers
- Be included in the community of men/women
- Develop partnership relationships
- Achieve mutual satisfaction
- Bring self and others back to joy simultaneously

Young adults: truth
- Discover the main characteristics of her/his own heart
- Develop a personal style that reflects his/her heart
- Proclaim her/his true identity
  - Personal identity
  - Corporate identity
  - Spiritual identity

Parent: gives sacrificially to children
- Needs
  - To give life without requiring anything back
  - An encouraging partner
  - Guidance from elders
  - Peer review from other fathers or mothers
  - A secure and orderly environment
- Tasks
  - Building a home
  - Protecting his or her family
  - Serving his or her family
  - Enjoying his or her family
  - Maturing their children
  - Synchronizing with the developing needs of: spouse, children, family, work and church

Parent: singles
- Single people and spiritual parenting
- If you have matured appropriately you have a group identity, so:
  - Start with extended family
  - Focus on same gender
  - Have parenting coaches
  - Get peer support and review to determine when and if ready for spiritual parenting

Parent: spiritual parents
- God forms the family
- Your community affirms the call and relationship
- Your elders guide you
- 3 levels of spiritual adoption:
  - Supplemental: assist parents
  - Stand In: acting as parent for a time
  - Replacement: replaces one or both parents
    - Singles proceed with great caution
    - Infants need 2 bonds for life, gender issues, and needs of the infant

THE BLUEPRINT FOR A NEW YOU!
MATURITY AND CAPACITY PART 2: THE STAGES OF MATURITY

Elders: grow their community
- Needs
  - A community to call their own
  - Recognition by their community
  - A proper place in the community structure
  - Have others place trust in him or her
- Tasks
  - Hospitality
  - Giving life to the family-less
  - Being a "parent" for the community itself
  - Maintain their community's identity
  - Still act like him/herself in the midst of difficulty
  - Enjoy what God placed in each and everyone
  - Build the trust of others through the elder's own transparency and spontaneity

What are the perils of ignoring maturity?

The 4 level emotional control center in the right hemisphere of the brain
- Immaturity is pain at Level 4

The perils of ignoring maturity
- For though by this time you ought to be teachers, you need some one to teach you again the first principles of God's word. You need milk, not solid food; for every one who lives on milk is unskilled in the word of righteousness, for he is a child. But solid food is for the mature, for those who have their faculties trained by practice to distinguish good from evil. Hebrews 5:12-14, RSV

The perils of ignoring maturity
- Leadership failure
- Character weakness
- Emotional instability
- Fearful living
  - Marriage failures
  - Failure to thrive
  - BEEPS (addictions)

BEEPS
- There are many different types of BEEPS. Examples can include:
  - Behaviors: Work
  - Events: Thrill Seeking
  - Experiences: Sex
  - People: Relationships
  - Substances: Alcohol

BEEPS are a catastrophic failure to reach adult maturity – and block the development of further maturity.

THE BLUEPRINT FOR A NEW YOU!
MATURITY AND CAPACITY PART 2: THE STAGES OF MATURITY

Trauma A: the absence of necessary good things

Trauma B: bad things that happen

Steps to restoring maturity
- Check for wounds in your identity
- Identify your level of earned maturity
- Identify the "holes" in your maturity
- Identity the "next step"
- Identify community resources you need
- Pray for God to provide the resources
- Start to work

The Twelve Steps are a relational program of recovery
- Relationship with God
  - Steps 1, 2, 3 and 11.
- Relationship with Self
  - Steps 4, 5, 6, 7 and 10.
- Relationship with Others
  - Steps 8, 9, and 12.
- Only when I work the Twelve Steps in a joyful, healing and maturing community can my maturity grow.

The "Thriving: Recover Your Life" training flow

Other modules in the Thriving: Recover Your Life training flow
- Belonging:
  - Thriving module for those who have completed Restarting or Forming
  - Helps build a joyful and thriving recovery community
  - Teaches the 19 skills the brain needs to thrive
- Forming:
  - Spiritual formation entrance to the Thriving training flow
  - Helps build a Christian character and identity that is joyful
- Healing
  - Designed for those who have completed Belonging
  - Continues the Immanuel Process that began in Restarting, Forming and Belonging
  - Helps participants experience the presence of God in a way that brings healing
  - Builds joyful and supportive healing community
- Loving
  - Designed for those who have completed the Healing module
  - Ongoing support for spiritual formation and recovery from trauma and BEEPS
  - Helps participants apply everything learned in other modules to relationships that are important to them
  - Following the completion of Loving, participants can identify relationships they would like to improve and repeat the entire Thriving process with those they love

THE BLUEPRINT FOR A NEW YOU!
MATURITY AND CAPACITY PART 2: THE STAGES OF MATURITY

EXERCISE: MATURITY ASSESSMENT *30 Minutes*

1. It is not necessary to break into small groups for the first part of this exercise.

2. Locate the maturity assessment in your workbook.

3. The purpose of this exercise is to help you assess your maturity and progress in developing the skills that are needed for infant and child levels of maturity. Listen as your facilitator explains:

   a. The assessment can help you celebrate and measure areas of growth. Over time, you will notice the growth of ongoing maturity.

   b. The assessment will help you answer the question, "What is my next step?" By helping you identify the areas in which you need to grow, you can begin to identify the resources, people and community that you need to mature.

   c. This assessment will help keep you safe. By recognizing your true level of maturity, you can avoid taking on responsibilities for which you do not have the maturity to handle.

   d. This assessment helps provide a blueprint for growth by identifying the tasks and challenges that are appropriate for your level of maturity.

   e. This assessment will help you identify gaps and holes in maturity that can keep you stuck and very frustrated. Gaps and holes in maturity can exist when we have not adequately mastered all of the skills needed at each level of maturity.

   f. This is a self-assessment exercise. You will not be asked to volunteer to share your assessment with anyone else.

4. Follow along on your assessment inventory as your facilitator explains how to complete the inventory.

   a. To the left side of the page are the words "No, Sometimes, Usually and Always." These help you describe the degree of progress you have made on specific maturity tasks.

   b. To the right, are a series of 5 basic infant tasks and 6 childhood tasks.

   c. The tasks are listed in bold.

   d. Below the tasks are a series of statements that describe the specific traits that must be developed to master the task.

   e. To complete the assessment, mark the "No, Sometimes, Usually or Always" box next to each statement.

5. Your facilitator will give you an example of how to complete the assessment.

   a. Find the task "Infant Lives in Joy" which is highlighted in bold on the first page of your assessment. It is the first task listed under the "Infant Stage" of maturity.

THE BLUEPRINT FOR A NEW YOU!
MATURITY AND CAPACITY PART 2: THE STAGES OF MATURITY

b. Find the statements "I am the same person over time" and "I know I am seen through the 'eyes of heaven.'"

c. Next to these statements are boxes for "No, Sometimes, Usually and Always."

d. Simply mark either the "No, Sometimes, Usually or Always" box that most accurately describes the statements, "I am the same person over time" and ""I know I am seen through the 'eyes of heaven.'"

   i. If you are not the same person over time, mark the "No" box.

   ii. If you are sometimes the same person over time, mark the "Sometimes" box.

   iii. If you are usually the same person over time, mark the "Usually" box.

   iv. It you are always the same person over time, mark the "Always" box.

e. You can complete the entire assessment in the same way.

6. This exercise is not asking you to base your answers solely on faulty or incomplete memories. It is asking you to determine whether you have the skills that are associated with an infant or child level of maturity in the present. Your facilitator will explain this example to you.

a. Locate the second infant maturity task "develops trust" that is highlighted in bold. The statement "Quiet time together helped calm myself with people around" is one of the traits listed below it.

b. If a person who is now 40 years old is unable to quiet and calm themselves with people around, it is unlikely that they learned this in biological infancy. They would mark the "No" box next to this statement, even if they can't remember their biological infancy.

c. If a person is now 40 years old, and usually is able to quiet and calm themselves with people around, they would mark the "Usually" box. They would mark the "Usually" box even if they can't remember learning this skill as a biological infant.

d. If a person is now 40 years old and learned this skill "Sometimes" at age 39, they would mark the "Sometimes" box, even if they can't remember their biological infancy.

e. The emphasis is on identifying skills that we have in the present – not trying to remember the distant past.

7. The ages listed on the assessment represent the earliest that it is possible for you to have developed all of the skills associated with a specific level of maturity. Your facilitator will explain:

a. Reaching a certain biological age does not mean that we have developed a corresponding level of maturity.

b. For example, a person may be 27 years old, but stuck at an infant level of maturity.

THE BLUEPRINT FOR A NEW YOU!
MATURITY AND CAPACITY PART 2: THE STAGES OF MATURITY

    c. They may remain stuck at that level of maturity until they are able to develop the skills and learn the tasks associated with that level of maturity.

    d. It is likely that a person who has experienced significant Trauma A, Trauma B and/or attachments to BEEPS may be stuck at an infant or child level of maturity.

8. This assessment helps you identify gaps or holes in maturity. Gaps or holes in maturity may happen when skills at a particular level of maturity are not adequately mastered. Even if other skills in that level of maturity are learned, gaps in maturity may remain if other skills at that level have been omitted – or insufficiently developed. Your facilitator will explain this example of a gap relating to anger at a childhood level of maturity:

    a. Find the infant skill, "Learns to return to joy from every negative emotion." Under it, you will see a list of the big six negative emotions. To develop an infant level of maturity, it is necessary to learn to return to joy from every negative emotion, including anger.

    b. If a person has not learned to return to joy from anger, but has learned every other infant level maturity task, they will have a gap in maturity associated with anger.

    c. They would function at a higher level of maturity in every area of life – except when they are angry. Their inability to return to joy from anger means that they would revert to an infant level of maturity when they are angry. They would be consumed with trying to protect themselves and make the pain stop – and would not be able to stay connected relationally to others when they are angry.

    d. The anger gap in maturity will also tend to sabotage efforts to develop skills at a child level of maturity. On your worksheet, locate the third child maturity task which is, "Develops enough persistence to do hard things." Below it are the traits, "I can do hard things I don't feel like doing" and "I can control my cravings."

    e. Being able to return to joy from anger is a prerequisite for developing these traits of childhood maturity. If I am unable to return to joy from anger, I will be unable to do hard things and control my cravings when I'm angry, because I'll be consumed with trying to protect myself and make my pain stop.

    f. This difficulty associated with childhood maturity tasks can only be resolved by addressing the underlying gaps at the infant level of maturity. Recognizing the gaps helps me get "unstuck," and identify the resources, community and people I need to mature.

9. Your facilitator will help you begin the assessment.

    a. Your facilitator will read each task and statement aloud, and will answer any questions that you may have.

THE BLUEPRINT FOR A NEW YOU!
MATURITY AND CAPACITY PART 2: THE STAGES OF MATURITY

b. Reflect on each statement, and mark "No, Sometimes, Usually or Always" next to each statement.

10. When you have completed the assessment, your facilitator will remind you that:

   a. You do not have to share your assessment with anyone.

   b. You can use your assessment to identify the gaps, and identify the resources, community and people that you need to mature.

   c. You can celebrate your progress, and return to the assessment again in the future as you mature.

CLOSE THE GROUP WITH PRAYER

MY MATURITY ASSESSMENT WORKSHEET

Follow your facilitator's instructions as you complete your worksheet.

No	Sometimes	Usually	Always	
				Infant stage: Ideal age: birth through age 4
				1. The infant lives in joy. The infant learns to expand their capacity for joy.
				The Infant also learns that joy is one's normal state and builds joy strength.
				a. I am the same person over time
				b. I know I am seen through the "eyes of heaven"
				2. Develops trust
				a. I have experienced strong loving bonds with mother or another woman.
				b. I have experienced strong loving bonds with father or another man.
				c. Important needs were met until I learned to ask.
				d. Quiet time together helped calm myself with people around.
				e. Others took the lead and synchronized with me and my feelings first.
				3. Learns how to receive
				a. I receive with joy and without guilt or shame.
				4. Begins to organize self into a person through relationship
				a. I know how to rest and quiet myself.
				b. I can receive and give life.
				c. I can now synchronize with others and their feelings.
				d. I found people to imitate so now I have a personality I like.
				5. Learns how to return to joy from every unpleasant emotion
				a. I learned how to regulate and quiet the big "six" emotions:
				1. Anger
				2. Fear
				3. Sadness
				4. Disgust
				5. Shame
				6. Hopelessness/Despair
				b. I can return to joy from every emotion and restore broken relationships
				1. Anger
				2. Fear
				3. Sadness
				4. Disgust
				5. Shame
				6. Hopelessness/Despair

MY MATURITY ASSESSMENT WORKSHEET

No	Sometimes	Usually	Always	
				Child Stage: Ideal age 4 through 12
				1. The child can ask for what is needed – can say what one thinks or feels
				a. I can ask for what I need.
				b. I enjoy self-expression.
				2. Learns what brings personal satisfaction
				a. I know what satisfies me.
				b. I can take care of myself.
				3. Develops enough persistence to do hard things
				a. I can do hard things I don't feel like doing.
				b. I can do hard things (even if they cause me some pain.)
				c. I am comfortable with reasonable risks, attempts and failures.
				d. I can control my cravings.
				4. Develop personal resources and talents
				a. I am growing in the things I am good at doing (my personal resources and talents)
				b. I have received love – I don't have to earn it.
				c. I can see myself through the "eyes of heaven".
				5. Knows self and takes responsibility to make self understood to others
				a. I help other people to understand me better if they don't respond well to me
				b. I can separate my feelings, my imagination and reality in my relationships
				6. Understand how she/he fits into history as well as "Big Picture" of what life is about
				a. I know how my family came to be the way it is in family history.
				b. I know how God's family came to be the way it is.
				c. I know the "Big Picture" of life with the stages of maturity.

THE BLUEPRINT FOR A NEW YOU!
MATURITY AND CAPACITY PART 2: THE STAGES OF MATURITY

QUESTIONS FOR FURTHER DISCUSSION OR FOLLOW-UP

1. What are the six stages of maturity? What are the earliest ages that it is possible to grow through each of these levels?

2. Why do you think that a community is needed for you to grow through each stage of maturity?

3. Are there infant level needs that have never been met in your life? What infant level tasks do you need to accomplish? List both the needs and tasks you still have.

4. Why is it so important to learn to do hard things that we don't feel like doing? Have you learned this skill? List some of the hard things you have learned to do.

5. Make a list of 7 things that are truly satisfying to you. Why is learning these things an essential aspect of recovery from trauma and BEEPS?

6. Are there child level needs that have never been met in your life? What child level tasks do you need to accomplish? List both the needs and tasks you still have.

7. Power, relationships and truth are very important to young adults. Why are these so important to them? What do they need to learn to develop proper use of these?

8. Learning to "protect others from yourself" is an important adult task. Why is this an important adult maturity task? Have you learned this task? Explain.

9. Why do parents need to give life without receiving anything back in order to grow into a parent level of maturity? Why is this a need – and not a task for parents?

10. What do single people need to function as spiritual parents? Where is a good place for them to start?

11. What are the 3 levels of spiritual adoption? Have you experienced – or do you need – adoption at one of these levels?

12. Why do you think that elders need community?

13. Do you know anyone who has reached an elder level of maturity? How do you feel when you are around them?

14. What are the perils of ignoring maturity? Have you experienced any of these? Explain.

15. Why are BEEPS the result of a failure to reach an adult level of maturity?

16. What are the next steps you need to take in your journey through recovery from trauma and BEEPS? Where are the community, resources and people that you need to take these steps? Be very specific.

THE BLUEPRINT FOR A NEW YOU!
MATURITY AND CAPACITY PART 2: THE STAGES OF MATURITY

OPTIONAL 12-STEP QUESTIONS

1. Why are attachments to BEEPS the result of a failure to reach an adult level of maturity?

2. What is your current level of maturity? How have trauma or attachments to BEEPS affected your maturity? Explain.

3. How do you define recovery? How do you define maturity?

4. What is the difference between recovery and maturity – or are they the same? Explain.

5. Can you grow in maturity without recovery from trauma and BEEPS?

6. Can you grow in recovery from trauma and BEEPS without maturity?

7. Do you think that maturity can be used to measure your growth in recovery? Why?

8. Do you think that relapse is related to maturity? Why?

9. Why do you need a mature community to grow in your recovery from BEEPS and trauma? What will happen to your recovery if you are not part of a healing community?

10. Do you think it is possible to grow in recovery if you only have relationships with others who have the same level of maturity as you? Explain.

11. How can my recovery grow if I work the Twelve Steps as part of a joyful, healing and mature community?

12. How would you like your relationships with God, self and others to mature as you grow in recovery? Be specific.

13. How is balanced growth in your relationship with God, self and others an important part of maturity? How can the Twelve Steps help you mature in these relationships?

14. Have you identified gaps or holes in your level of maturity? Where are the resources, community and people that you need to grow in your maturity and recovery?

15. What are the "next steps" that you need to take to grow in maturity and recovery?

THRIVING RECOVER YOUR LIFE
HOW DO THE FIVE THRIVING MODULES WORK TOGETHER?

MODULES

Restarting

Restarting is the entry module for the *Thriving: Recover Your Life* program. Over a 12 week period, in Restarting groups you learn how you are created for joy. You learn how to recognize where your brain lacks joy and how to connect with others in order to retrain your brain FOR JOY! Restarting groups combine joy building exercises, DVD teachings from Ed Khouri and this workbook full of notes, follow up questions and 12 Step applications for training. Each class is one third teaching and two thirds exercises! Restarting is all about retraining the brain, not just understanding why we are the way we are!

Forming

Thriving is for the whole church. Forming is an entrance to the Thriving: Recover your life program for people who want to grow their spiritual maturity by engaging at deeper levels with God. This 12 week module is all about forming your relationship with Jesus! In Forming, you will learn more about hearing God and finding your true identity in Christ. You will begin to see yourself through the eyes of heaven and recognize grace as an active force for change.

Belonging

Your second 90 days take you through the Belonging module. You will work in small groups to restore your ability to create a joyful place for others to belong with you. Belonging jump-starts your process of learning the 19 skills that build healthy relationships and strong emotional resilience. In Belonging you learn to recognize when your relational circuits are off and get them running again. Creating belonging means learning not to overwhelm others, recognizing the effects of attachment pain and learning a surprising way to control your cravings.

Healing

Healing is the module where you can discover how to experience Jesus in the painful places of life. Jesus is the healer, and by the time participants get to this module, they have built up enough joy capacity to let Jesus do His work! We work on inner healing in the safety of groups of 3 to 5 and begin each exercise with God in a joyful situation! In Healing, we will learn to distinguish God's voice from our own. This module will utilize the Immanuel Process developed in connection with Dr. Karl Lehman.

Loving

Loving is the last module in Thriving: Recover Your Life. In this module you will take what you have learned in all the previous modules and apply it to your own relationships. You will take the joy and healing that you have been developing back to the relationships that God has placed in your life. You will practice receiving and giving good things to the people you live with and love - or wish you could.

WHAT COMES NEXT?
RESTARTING

Your second 90 days

When you have completed Restarting in your first 90 days, you are ready for the next module in the Thriving: Recover Your Life Program, which is called Belonging. In Belonging, you will be able to spend 3 months continuing to build joy and growing in recovery and relationship skills. Belonging is training for your brain's control system. You will learn:

- How can I create a place for others to belong in joy around me...and develop life-giving relationships?

- How do I experience appreciation and self-quieting.

- What keeps me alone – and keeps me from creating a place for others to belong with me?

- How can I keep the relational part of my brain working so that I am able to actually connect with God and others.

- How can I practically restore my relational circuits if they are not working well?

- Why do people like – or hate – me, and what can I do about it?

- How do I recognize and deal with the pain that makes me relapse into addictive or abuse driven behaviors...before I relapse?

- What are the skills I need to make my cravings stop in their tracks?

- How can I see my life and others like God does?

- What do I do when I feel overwhelmed by others so that I calm down quickly?

- How can I learn to respond well to others...and not overwhelm or ignore them?

Your third 90 days

Your third 90 days you will be spend in the Healing module. You need time to learn to heal. This training helps you experience the presence of God in a way that helps you heal from the devastating effects of addictions, trauma, neglect and abuse. In Healing, you will work in small groups to continue to learn and practice the Immanuel Process. You will discover:

- How can I connect with God to talk with Him about my pain?

- How can unhappy memories silently block my awareness of God?

- What steps can I take to resolve these problems?

- Why does God want to connect with me anyway?

- What can I do when I get stuck working through something painful in my life?

- How can I learn to help others begin to talk with God about their pain?

- How can I learn to have a more stable identity, even when things are going wrong?

- How can we as a group all heal, grow and move forward in joy together?

Finishing your first year in recovery – the last 90 days

The Loving module will help you to apply practically all you have learned in the Thriving Program. Your focus is growing relationships with the people in your life that you care about the most. You will work on the skills needed to:

- Build relationships that help my recovery.

- Remove the fear that keeps me from relating to those closest to me.

- Create a place for those I care about to belong with me in joy.

- Know how attachment pain has kept me from relating to those I care about.

- Know what do when relationships don't heal.

- Continue to connect with God to resolve ongoing pain in my relationships.